HOW TO MAKE
CLASSIC
WOODEN TOYS

ISBN 978-1-4971-0466-2

The Cataloging in Publication Data is on file with the Library of Congress.

Managing Editor: Gretchen Bacon

Acquisitions Editor: Kaylee J. Schofield

Editor: Joseph Borden

Designers: Ines Freire / Alfons Freire

Proofreader: Jeremy Hauck

Indexer: Jay Kreider

Photo Credits: p. 26— Akeneo Courtesy of JPW Industries; pp. 1, 4, 5, 30, 31, 33, 37, 41, 45, 49, 53, 57, 61, 65, 71, 75, 79, 85, 91, 97— Mike Mihalo Photography.

Shutterstock Images: p. 10 (brad point bit)— Chase Somero, (Forstner bit)— Aleksey Mnogosmyslov, (twist bit)— /New Africa; p. 11 (band saw)—/gualtiero boffi; p. 12 (planer)—Olef, (spring clamps)— hardvicore; p. 15 (maple)—/Pawel Hankus, (cherry)—/Tony Savino, (oak)—Yosuke8, (walnut)— Guiyuan Chen, (poplar)—Alberto Sebastiani, (pine)—Efetova Anna.

To learn more about the other great books from Fox Chapel Publishing, or to find a retailer near you, call toll-free at 800-457-9112 or visit us at www.FoxChapelPublishing.com.
You can also send mail to:
Fox Chapel Publishing
903 Square Street
Mount Joy, PA 17552

We are always looking for talented authors. To submit an idea, please send a brief inquiry to acquisitions@foxchapelpublishing.com.

Printed in China
First printing

HOW TO MAKE
CLASSIC
WOODEN TOYS

Woodworkers' Plans for 15 Sturdy Toys That Go
Plus Skill-Building Techniques

BRAD ANDERSON

FOX CHAPEL
PUBLISHING

Contents

32

48

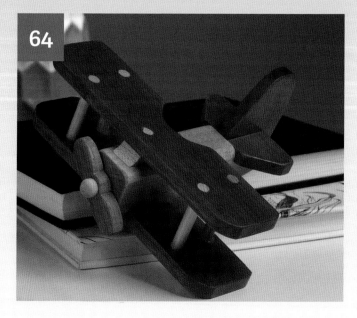

64

40

44

52

60

84

96

Getting Started

Toy-making requires a solid understanding of the materials and tools essential for creating durable and enjoyable toys. This section will introduce you to the basics from selecting the right wood to understanding the design process. I'll ensure you have a practical foundation to start crafting toys that are both safe and functional.

Toy Design

Designing toys is my favorite part of the process. The most important thing to keep in mind when designing toys for children is that toys are meant to be tough and built for play, not just for display.

My inspiration for toy ideas comes from various sources, but most often, my designs are based on real vehicles. Once I have an idea, I research the project. I conduct image searches to get a better understanding of the key features of my subject. Then, I move on to hand sketches, outlining concept drawings with some rough dimensions and constraints.

When I'm comfortable with my sketches, I transition to CAD (Computer-Aided Design) software for a more detailed design. I've used a variety of CAD tools, including Fusion 360, SketchUp, Autodesk Inventor, and SolidWorks. Each has its pros and cons, but the primary goal is to ensure that all the toy's pieces fit together seamlessly. This step helps me figure out how to make the parts, assemble the toy, and get a sense of the final size.

It's where I find answers to design questions that I thought about while researching the toy.

While designing parts in a CAD program, I make sure to design them as they would be made in a woodshop, because these programs can sometimes create parts that are challenging or impossible to machine or drill. Each part starts as a blank piece, then is cut and drilled as it would be done in the shop. Once the design is complete, I create plans for each part, aiming to keep them sized to fit on a standard sheet of paper. These plans serve as templates for making the toys and undergo testing and revisions as needed. As I make these designs for the first time, I make notes on the plans and adjust the designs until I'm satisfied.

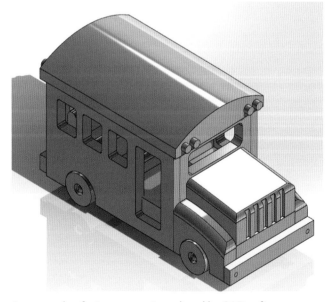

An example of a toy concept rendered by CAD software.

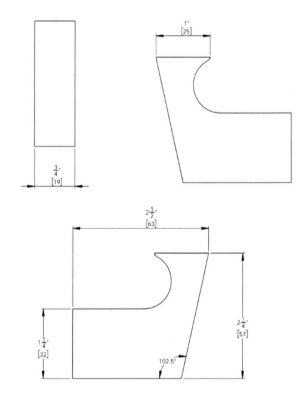

When designing toy pieces, I aim to size them to fit on a standard sheet of paper and ensure they are easy to cut and drill.

Patterns vs. Templates

When working with patterns, I start by making two copies of the drawings. The first set serves as my reference and is stapled together. This helps keep me on track during the woodworking project, and I take notes of the process or things I have learned. The second set is used for creating patterns or templates. When I'm making multiples of the same toy, I often use cardstock paper templates, which are easy to make.

Many parts will not need a pattern or template to be made. There are several parts where the dimensions can be taken from the part drawing and copied to the part blank. These parts usually have minimal work to make them, as with the chassis. When the part is difficult or has curves, it is easier to put the pattern on the wood itself.

Patterns

Transferring precise dimensions, especially curves and arcs, to a blank can be challenging. Using patterns glued directly to the wood is often more efficient. Start by making a copy of the pattern and checking that the dimensions are accurate. If not, adjust the printer/copier settings to ensure there is proper scaling.

To attach the pattern, first cut it out, then apply a layer of painter's tape to the wood. Use spray adhesive to glue the pattern to the tape, which allows for easy removal later.

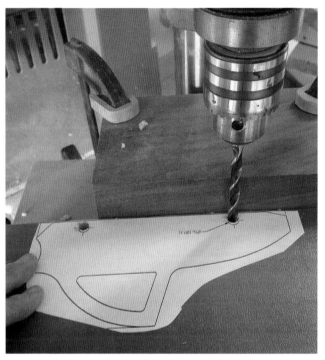

For more intricate projects, affix a pattern directly to your workpiece to ensure you cut the correct dimensions.

Templates

When I am making many copies of one toy, I use a more robust material to make a template to trace onto the part. I often use ⅛" (3mm) hardboard or thin scrap stock, which lasts longer than the cardstock templates. To create a template, simply cut a piece of thin material to match the size of the part you're working on. Next, glue the pattern onto the hardboard and proceed to cut the template out on the scroll saw. These templates have a notable advantage: they are reusable and can make more than one part. Though they may be a bit weightier and less convenient to attach to the drawings, they significantly outlast the lighter cardstock templates.

Attaching parts by using a pin nail is a more reliable way to prevent them from coming loose.

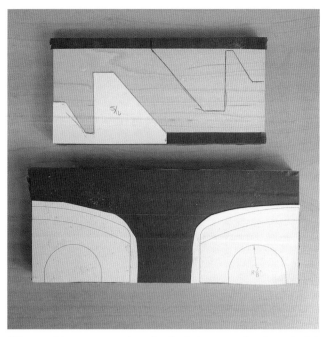

When making many copies of a single toy, use a hardy material to make a template you can reuse.

If the templates require holes, I do not drill the actual size. I drill a ⅛" (3mm) hole in the center and use a nail set or awl to make an indentation where the hole is supposed to go.

Relative Dimensions

When it comes to reading plans, remember that they are excellent for conveying ideas, and they are most effective when all the parts are made with precision. This is where the concept of relative dimensioning comes into play. It's a practical approach that ensures the parts fit together seamlessly. Instead of fixating on achieving absolute precision in dimensions, keep in mind that these are toys, not fine furniture. The crucial aspect is to ensure the pieces fit well together, ensuring safe and enjoyable playtime experiences.

Tools

One aspect of making toys is that you don't need a workshop filled with fancy tools. While various tools can make the process easier, the essential toolkit for making toys can be divided into three categories: hand tools, power tools, and additional tools.

Power Tools

Table saw. The table saw is the workhorse in my shop. I use it for cutting blanks and grooving. You can use a benchtop saw, but I find the cabinet saw superior if you will be making many projects. Cabinet saws have better fences and can accommodate a dado stack, which is necessary for the projects in this book.

Push blocks. It is important to keep hands and fingers away from the blade. The push stick is good, but it does not work when cutting strips less than ⅜" (9.5mm) wide. This is where push blocks come in handy.

Table Saw Safety Tips

- Ensure the fence and blade are parallel for safe rip cuts.
- Set the fence to the correct distance for the cut width.
- Make sure the riving knife or blade guard is in place.
- Use a push stick for cuts less than 4" (102mm).
- For crosscuts, use the miter gauge and move the fence to avoid kickback.
- Kickback occurs when the material binds between the blade and fence, so keep this area clear.
- Attach a reference block to the fence in front of the blade for consistent cuts and to prevent binding.

Here, I'm using a miter gauge to provide stability while crosscutting.

Miter gauge. This makes angled cuts easier and can also provide more stability when crosscutting.

Miter saw. These are used to cut angles and crosscut pieces to a consistent length. They easily handle long pieces with additional support, making batching parts quick, but aren't safe for cutting small pieces under 3" (76mm). To cut angled backs (like on a race car or Model T), set the miter saw angle, cut lengths slightly longer than needed, and trim to size with a scroll saw. For identical parts, set a stop block to cut pieces to the same length. Avoid forcing material against the stop block, as this can shift it and cause inconsistencies.

Scroll saw. The scroll saw allows me to add details and contours to the toy designs. For the designs in this book, a high-end scroll saw is not required I recommend getting a scroll saw that uses a pinless blade. The internal cutouts are large and there are no intricate designs to cut out. If you are looking to do more intricate designs, research the different brands of saws and the difference between pinned and pinless blades. (See Introduction to Scroll Saws on page 28.)

Router. The router has many different uses and abilities. I use it to profile parts (soften the hard edges). A powerful router is not needed for these toys and may be harder to use. The important part is that it is mounted to a table, and you are not freehand routing parts. I will always make my parts oversized for the router. The tops of the fenders are all routed, so I cut a longer piece and adhere the pattern to the piece. I cut out where the profile is to be cut and then profile the part before cutting it completely out. This is shown in the profiling of the fenders for the bus. This keeps the part larger so it is easier to hold or use a push pad. I also use the router to ease the inside edges of windows and cutouts. I use a ⅛" (3mm) roundover bit to ease the back side of cut outs.

Drill press. The drill press drills the holes for your wheels and dowels. It is important that it is able to drill straight and make repeatable actions. I have been able to do most of the drilling on my benchtop drill press. The success of your drill press mostly comes down to setup. I have a 2" (51mm) square block of wood that clamps to the table of the drill press to drill holes square to the face of the part. I clamp stop blocks if I am drilling more than one piece with the same hole pattern.

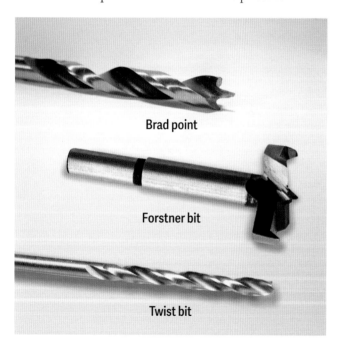

Brad point

Forstner bit

Twist bit

Drill bits. I use three different drill bits: bradpoints, twist bits, and Forstner bits. *Brad points* have a point on the end that keeps the bit from walking. This type of drill bit is mainly used in wood and other soft materials. *Twist bits* self-center, which is useful when drilling a hole deeper for assembly dowel holes or making a hole larger. This bit can

also be used on metal. I have a set of brad points and twist bits from ⅛" (3mm) to ½" (13mm) in ¹⁄₆₄" (0.4mm) increments. This allows me to drill an appropriate diameter of the hole if the peg or dowel are slightly larger or smaller. *Forstner bits* create a cleaner hole and are usually used for holes that are greater than ½" (13mm) or need to have clean sides and a flat bottom. This bit is used in the tugboat for the smokestack and cabin window.

Hand Tools

Clamps. Clamps are indispensable for holding parts together while the glue dries. Having a good selection of 6" (150mm) and 12" (300mm) clamps is essential. You don't need to clamp pieces super tight; trigger-type clamps work well. Spring clamps are also useful in adding smaller and accent pieces to the toys.

Hammer. A small hammer or a rubber mallet comes in handy for driving in axle pegs and dowels. An 8oz (230g) hammer is suitable for this task.

Sandpaper. Sandpaper is a must. It's used to smooth out rough surfaces and break sharp edges, ensuring your toys are safe to play with. Consider using sanding sponges for contours and inside edges. A grit sequence of 100, 150, and 220 is commonly used. Sanding is an ongoing process, from initial assembly to final finish.

used to cut most of the parts for the projects in this book. (See Introduction to Band Saws on page 26.)

Chisel and hand plane. These tools can be useful for refining grooves and smoothing out saw marks. These tools can also add details and break edges on an assembly, like the chamfer on the cross beam of the jeep. Planers also allow you to make the boards the thickness you want them and can help remove imperfections like a slight bow or inconsistent thickness.

Additional Tools

While the tools mentioned so far cover the basics, the following are not strictly necessary, but they can enhance efficiency and ease in toy making.

Drum and belt sanders. These tools expedite sanding and are useful for cleaning up glue lines and achieving smoother surfaces. I typically use 150-grit sandpaper with these.

Band saw. A is a great tool for resawing boards into thinner stock, saving you from buying thin stock materials. It is also useful in cutting the angles on the engine for the tow truck. In fact, a band saw can be

Airbrush and air compressor. If you're finishing a lot of toys, an airbrush and air compressor provide better control and efficiency compared to spray cans. They can save you money on paint purchases.

Measuring and Marking Tools

A sharp **pencil** is the simplest way of marking dimensions and hole locations on the parts. It leaves clear, easy-to-follow lines and works wonderfully on a wide range of wood types. For lighter woods, you might consider using a 0.7mm **mechanical pencil** to maintain a fine point. For darker woods, such as walnut and cherry, I like to use a **white gel pen**. It contrasts well with the wood, ensuring your marks are visible.

A reliable **tape measure** is a simple yet indispensable tool for measuring and marking the dimensions of your wooden pieces. A **ruled square** allows you to make consistent marks, a critical aspect when marking axle and peg holes. These tools are the key to ensuring parts fit together seamlessly.

Planer. This will allow you to make the boards the thickness you want them. It can help remove imperfections like a slight bow or inconsistent thickness. It is good to ensure all the boards are the same thickness. Pictured here is a simple manual planer, but powered options are available, as well.

Clamps

You don't need fancy, large clamps to create awesome toys. My top three go-to clamps are quick-release clamps, spring-clamps, and rubber bands—simple, but super effective in toy-making.

Quick-release clamps. Also known as trigger-style bar clamps, these are like the Swiss Army knife of woodworking clamps. They are not as strong as other kinds of clamps, but you usually don't need that much clamping force when assembling toys. Plus, they're easy to handle with just one hand. They are perfect for setting up temporary fixtures to join parts together and clamping stop blocks to fences.

Spring clamps. These work like clothespins. They might not have the strength to close big gaps, but they're perfect for bringing two pieces together, like the hulls of a tugboat. They're also handy for clamping spacers and stops to fences.

Rubber bands. These are not exactly a clamp, but they're the heroes of holding irregular pieces together. I use rubber bands to keep the tail section attached to the fuselage of a biplane while the glue dries.

Basics of Wood

Wood selection plays an important role in ensuring the longevity and safety of the toy. Hardwoods are less likely to dent and chip during play, providing increased durability. Softwoods are more prone to denting and may not withstand extended use. Avoid softwoods if there's any possibility of a child putting the toys in their mouth, as they can be a safety concern. It's important that the wood used is clean and untreated. Reclaimed lumber, especially from pallets, can contain heat treatments or chemicals that simple planing may not completely remove.

While exotic lumber can add color and uniqueness to a toy, it's crucial to assess unfamiliar or new woods for toxicity and other characteristics. For example, wenge tends to splinter easily, so any dents or chips could potentially result in splinters. Iroko is considered a sensitizer and may cause rashes and respiratory issues. Walnut, which is one of my favorite woods, can cause reactions for people with tree nut allergies. Information on the toxicity and characteristics of wood can easily be found online.

Grain Direction

The grain and grain direction in the wood can strengthen the toy. Joints where the end grain connects to the face grain are generally weaker unless reinforced with fasteners or alternative forms of joinery. Additionally, it's easier to break a board along the grain than across it.

There are methods to fortify toy parts to minimize the need for repairs. Please consider these design features for the projects in this book:

- The arms on the skid loader were initially designed as a single piece, but they frequently broke along the grain where they connected to the bucket. To strengthen this piece, I used a groove and dowel joint. While it made the production process slightly more challenging, it eliminated the issue of breakage.

- The top dowels on the jeep are inserted deeply into the sides to strengthen the narrow area of the car's sides. Dowels are also used to strengthen joints being glued together. This adds a natural fastener so the glue joint does not break.

- The four exhaust pieces on the jet serve a dual purpose: they provide added surface area for gluing the wings to the body, enhancing the bond, and they strengthen the wings themselves. These considerations are crucial, as some children may test the toy's flying abilities, even though it's not designed to fly or glide gracefully. The orientation of the grain in the exhaust pieces creates a cross-grain bond like plywood, reinforcing the wings and facilitating a more secure glue bond with the body.

Understanding Wood Characteristics

When I first started woodworking, I would go through the entire stock of wood at the big box store to find the perfect board, straight with no defects. I did not find many perfect boards. Over time, I have learned that not all defects are unusable, and many can be cut out so parts can

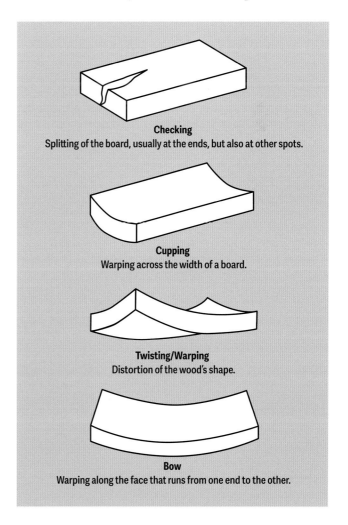

Checking
Splitting of the board, usually at the ends, but also at other spots.

Cupping
Warping across the width of a board.

Twisting/Warping
Distortion of the wood's shape.

Bow
Warping along the face that runs from one end to the other.

be made from them. Here, I have listed several common defects and how to work with them.

- **Bow.** When wood has a bow, it means it deviates from being perfectly straight along the grain. In such cases, you don't have a straight edge as a reference for ripping the lumber to a uniform width. To tackle this, you can cut the board into smaller pieces, which can help reduce the bow and allow you to safely cut a straight reference edge on the wood piece. If the board exhibits a significant bow, consider using it for parts of your project that don't require a straight reference edge. This approach works well for components in projects like the tugboat and race car.

- **Cup.** Cupping is somewhat like bowing, but it happens across the grain of the wood. It's a bit of a challenge to work with because the board isn't flat on the table, and there's a risk of kickback when using a table saw. To address cupping, you can plane the wood flat, which reduces its thickness. Afterward, you can use the flat board for the thinner parts of your project.

- **Checks/splits.** These are imperfections that usually occur at the ends of the wood and must be removed. Checks and splits are ways in which wood relieves internal stresses. However, if you spot cracks and splits in the middle of a board, that's a sign of more significant stress or damage. It's best to avoid boards with these mid-section checks.

- **Knots.** Knots are defects that often form where tree branches once were. The great thing about making toys is that the parts are relatively small, making it easier to simply cut around and remove this defect. However, knots can sometimes be intentionally included in a part if they are solid, firmly in place, and without any loose parts or cracks. Knots are denser than the surrounding wood, adding a unique character. Still, it's not recommended to drill into them or cut through them, as they can be tough to work with.

- **Twist/warp.** When a board exhibits a twist or warp, it means the two ends of the board don't

lie in the same plane, and the board may have multiple bends or curves. In the view of many woodworkers, if a board has a significant twist, it's essentially unusable or will generate a lot of waste in material if you try to make it usable.

Choosing the Right Wood for Your Project

Wood selection is a critical aspect of crafting toys. It can determine the success and durability of your creation, both in a literal and figurative sense. Here are some key factors to consider when selecting wood:

- **Cleanliness.** First and foremost, the wood you choose must be clean. Exercise caution when considering recycled or reclaimed wood. Chemicals might have penetrated deep into the wood, making it less suitable for toy making. As a result, materials like pallet wood or wood that has had a stain or paint on them are generally not recommended for toys. However, due to the small size of most toys, you can work with boards that have imperfections. You can inquire at a lumber yard if they have shorter pieces of wood with defects that they can sell at a reduced price.

- **Qualities.** Not all wood has the same qualities, and different regions produce different trees that have adapted to their environment. It is important to review the qualities and any health implications that may occur when using a given lumber. Most of my knowledge relates to domestic species in the United States. There is a lot of information online about the toxicology of different wood species, and I encourage you to review this information when trying new woods in toys.

- **Durability.** It's highly recommended to opt for hardwoods due to their durability. They can withstand the wear and tear of playtime. Domestic hardwoods are a practical choice because they come in various thicknesses, making them versatile for toy-making. These woods are capable of enduring vigorous use. Exotic woods are less commonly used, primarily due to their cost. Some exotic woods may also pose health hazards, so review information online about the wood species you are using.

Common Woods

Maple. Typically exhibits a light, creamy color with occasional reddish-brown streaks. Maple is known for its fine, consistent grain, making it easy to work with and finish. It takes well to paint and stains. It is a hardwood, so it's reasonably durable. It falls into a mid-range price category, making it a good choice for quality toys.

Cherry. Starts with a pale, pinkish-brown hue and deepens to a rich, reddish-brown over time. It often features a warm, reddish tone. It is easy to work with, offering a smooth texture and fine grain. It is considered a premium hardwood, and it's somewhat more expensive.

Oak. Known for its golden to medium brown color, with prominent grain patterns. Oak can be a bit tougher to work with due to its grain, but it still offers good workability. It is widely available and moderately priced. It's a popular choice for various woodworking projects.

Walnut. Boasts a rich, dark brown to black color with attractive grain patterns. Walnut works a lot like cherry and finishes well. Walnut is considered a high-quality hardwood and is more expensive. Its striking appearance and ease of use make it great to add accent color to toys.

Poplar. Generally light in color, ranging from creamy white to pale green or yellow. It is known for being soft and easy to work with. It is on the softer side, so it is prone to dents when played with. It can be painted and finished easily. Poplar is often more affordable compared to hardwoods like maple, cherry, or walnut. It's a practical choice for cost-effective projects.

Pine. Typically light yellow to pale reddish-brown with distinctive knots. Pine is soft and easy to work with. Its character comes from its knots and grain. There is a higher waste factor because of the knots. It is usually among the most affordable. Clear pine can also be used but comes at a premium price.

These are the majority of woods I work with in the United States. Other areas of the world will have different domestic hardwoods. Each wood type has its unique characteristics, making it suitable for various toy-making projects. Consider your budget, project requirements, and desired aesthetics when making your wood selection.

General Woodworking Terminology

When you are new to woodworking, you may come across many terms that can make the directions hard to understand. Below is a list of terms to make it easier to follow along with the projects from this book.

Blank size. Consider this the initial size of your raw material. It's the minimum amount of wood you need to craft a specific part. The blank might be the exact size of the component—like chassis and square parts—or occasionally, you could start with a larger blank for ease of machining or for safety reasons, as seen in the construction of the tugboat's hull.

Rip cut. A rip cut involves slicing a board along its grain, essentially lengthwise. This is typically done with a table saw and a fence. It's ideal for adjusting the width of your piece.

Crosscut. When you crosscut, you're essentially cutting across the wood grain, perpendicular to it. A miter saw is commonly used for this, but you can also achieve it with a table saw and miter gauge or by hand. Crosscuts are all about achieving the correct length for your piece.

Angled cuts. These are cuts that deviate from the standard perpendicular orientation. Miter saws are often employed for making angled cuts. When working on projects such as race cars or Model Ts, it is better to perform all the angled cuts with the same setup for consistency.

Stop block. Think of a stop block as a precision tool you secure at a specific location to ensure uniform cuts and drillings. You'll commonly find them in use with miter saws and drill presses. They come in handy when producing multiple identical items or when you need holes to align perfectly. For example, using stop blocks can ensure that holes in your Model T or pickup truck roof match up precisely with the holes in the sides.

Rabbet (rebate). Rabbet is a joinery technique that involves cutting a recess in the edge of a board. This recess helps in aligning and supporting the adjoining piece, ensuring a squared-up connection.

Dado. Dado is another joinery technique that creates a groove in a board, providing support to the adjoining piece on three sides. It's typically executed on a table saw using a dado stack or by making multiple passes with a regular table saw blade. Alternatively, you can use a router to create dados.

Counterbore holes. This process consists of two steps. First, you use a Forstner bit to drill a larger hole partially through the wood. Then, a smaller diameter bit completes the drilling process through the piece. The use of a twist-style bit for the second hole is preferred because it centers on the mark left by the Forstner bit. The outcome is a recess that accommodates a peg, ensuring a snug fit in the part. This technique is especially valuable in making projects like the skid loader.

Finishes

When it comes to finishing your wooden toys, ensuring they're safe for children is important. Different countries have specific regulatory requirements. For instance, in the United States, the FDA has regulations regarding food-safe finishes. In Europe, they have the Toy Safe Certification (EN-71) to ensure toy finishes meet safety standards. If your toy is for a child who might chew on it or put it in their mouth, make sure the finish is considered food-grade safe. For other toys, a nontoxic finish should suffice. If you have any doubts, it's a good idea to consult the manufacturer of the finish and review current regulations.

The toys in this book are not designed as teethers or toys that can be put in a child's mouth. There are small parts that do present a choking hazard. For this reason, I do not make teethers and my scrap blocks are left unifinished. **I do not recommend any of these toys for kids under three years old.**

Here are some simple guidelines:

- Avoid finishes that contain heavy metals like lead and cadmium.

- Steer clear of metallic paints.

- Never use oils that can spoil or go rancid, such as cooking oils.

There are three main finishing techniques we'll explore. Each has its own set of pros and cons. You must determine what works best for you.

Leave the Toy Unfinished

This is the easiest solution, and it ensures there are no chemicals added to the toy. It's a genuinely non-toxic finish. There are advantages to leaving the toy unfinished.

It maintains the natural aesthetic of the wood and it is environmentally friendly. Plus, you won't have to worry about fixing paint or reapplying finish. However, keep in mind that leaving a toy unfinished might raise some concerns about durability. Wood can swell when exposed to moisture, which may cause moving parts to stick. Cleaning an unfinished toy can be challenging since dirt and liquids can be absorbed into the wood. There's also a slight concern about walnut dust potentially triggering allergic reactions. So, while leaving the wood toy in a natural, unfinished state is the easiest and safest option, it does come with some considerations.

Oils

There are several natural oils suitable for finishing toys. Some popular ones are tung oil, polymerized linseed oil, and walnut oil. Oils penetrate the toy, preventing water and dirt absorption. They don't create a film finish. However, be cautious about additives in the oils that may be harmful to children. I stick to the food-grade finishing oils. Oils bring out the wood's grain and natural colors, provide protection against moisture, and prevent the wood from drying out and cracking.

Pictured here are two popular food-safe finishes: tung oil and raw linseed oil. If you decide to finish with linseed oil, be sure that it is raw, not boiled. Boiled linseed oil is toxic.

Application is usually straightforward, and repairs can be made if needed. The downside is that oil finishes take time to dry, sometimes up to 30 days. Some oils never cure, like mineral oil. The oils do not build up a protective layer but penetrate into the wood. They may also need periodic reapplication and can attract dust, making cleaning a bit challenging.

Beeswax and carnauba wax can also be used as finishes. These take a little more work than traditional oil and film finishes. The wax needs to be worked into the toy and then buffed out. When done correctly, it leaves a beautiful finish.

Film Finishes

Film finishes dry quickly, allowing for multiple coats in a short timeframe. I find these best for toys.

These finishes create a protective layer over the wood, bringing out its natural colors and grain. They shield the wood from quickly absorbing liquids and moisture and are easy to clean. Film finishes dry faster, allowing for multiple coats over several days. They can vary from matte to high gloss, depending on wood type and surface preparation. You usually won't need to reapply the finish unless the toy needs to be repaired. However, applying and repairing film finishes can be a bit trickier. They often have a strong odor, so an organic filter respirator is recommended. They also typically don't have water-based cleanup, unless stated on the container. These finishes include polyurethane and shellac.

My go-to finish is shellac because I can do multiple coats in one day. The premade shellac runs great through my airbrush, so I do not have to worry about thinning and diluting it. Shellac is also found naturally. I have also used polyurethane on toys. After I started using an airbrush, the polyurethane needed to be thinned out a little to flow correctly.

In conclusion, there are numerous options for finishing your toys, and your choice will depend on your preferences, research, and priorities. As for me, I prefer to use shellac as a final coat on the toys I make. It flows nicely through an airbrush, and it's a natural substance.

Adhesives

The two common adhesive choices for toy construction are wood glue and cyanoacrylate (CA) glue. Each is distinguished by unique attributes tailored to specific applications.

Please note wood glue and CA glue are not designed for gap filling. Surface preparation is a prerequisite before bonding two pieces of wood together. The pieces should fit together with no gaps. Clamping out the gap may work in the short term, but could have an effect on durability and ease of assembling the other pieces together. I have found that if I try to clamp out a gap or bow, it will show when all wheels don't touch the floor.

Wood glue is the primary adhesive in toy fabrication. Characterized by a denser viscosity and an extended open time of approximately 10–15 minutes, this adhesive affords a window to make small adjustments during the clamping phase. Once cured, the bond is stronger than the wood itself.

CA glue is valued for its swift bonding and fast drying capabilities. When paired with an accelerator, the bond practically forms in the blink of an eye, resulting in a significantly shorter open time. With its very thin viscosity, CA glue excels at bonding joints after they've been assembled, a technique often applied when attaching wheels to a tractor harrow. Additionally, CA glue proves invaluable for repairs, especially in addressing issues like blowouts and chipped corners.

CA glue should not be used as a primary glue for woodworking projects. It is a very thin glue, which

---

TIP

Part of woodworking is knowing how to fix mistakes. There have been more times than I would like to admit when I have glued something in the wrong place, or it has shifted. If it is caught before 30–45 minutes after the clamps have been set, there is a chance the part can be salvaged. Microwave the part for 20–30 seconds. Gently wedge the two pieces apart with a chisel. This is not guaranteed to work, but it may save a part.

allows wood to absorb it quickly and not bond to the other piece. It also is more brittle, making it more prone to breaking at the joints than wood glue. I use CA glue for quick repairs, such as filling an accidental hole.

Glue and Finishes

It is crucial to note that wood glue does not bond with finishes. There are times when it is easier to finish the part either separately or in subassemblies. You should tape off sections that should remain unfinished, complete the finishing process, and then peel off the tape and glue the unfinished parts for the final assembly. The roof and top of the bus is taped off while it is being finished because it is easier to finish the inside with the roof off. After finishing, the tape is removed, and the roof is glued in place.

Gluing Blocks

Gluing pieces together to make a larger block can be messy. I have used both fingers and pieces of wood to spread an even layer of glue. I was introduced to the silicon brush a few years back and highly recommend it. Using fingers leaves fingerprints on the wood and leads to a lot of sanding. Using wood to spread glue also creates a mess. The silicon brush makes it easy to create a thin film of glue on the part. You can leave a silicon brush on a piece of paper and let it dry. After it is dry, the glue can be peeled off and the brush can be reused.

General Safety

Working with wood and using tools carries inherent risks, and it's crucial to minimize these risks to a level that makes you feel comfortable. Confidence and comfort are paramount when crafting these toys. If you have any concerns about a task, consider alternative methods or tools to achieve a similar result. For example, you can use sandpaper instead of a router to profile an edge, clamp a workpiece to a drill press instead of holding it by hand, or modify the design to better accommodate the tools in your workshop.

In this section, I will discuss some general safety considerations for a safe and enjoyable scrolling experience, as well as considerations particular to cutting the toys featured in this book.

Personal Protective Equipment (PPE)

When it comes to personal protective equipment (PPE), remember that some protection is always better than none. In this section, we will look into essential PPE designed to safeguard your eyes, hearing, and respiratory health. It's imperative to prioritize safety, and there should be no excuses for not wearing PPE.

Eye Protection

Safety glasses are essential for eye protection and should meet at least ANSI Z87 standards. Look for lenses that wrap around the sides of your head. Regular sunglasses and prescription glasses without the ANSI Z87 stamp don't qualify. Goggles can be worn over prescription glasses, or prescription glasses can be made to meet ANSI specs. Safety glasses are widely available in stores and online. In humid environments,

Safety glasses should meet ANSI Z87 standards to ensure adequate protection.

use anti-fog spray for clarity. Ensure a snug fit so they stay secure without obstructing your view.

Hearing Protection

OSHA (Occupational Safety and Health Administration, a US government agency) requires hearing protection in workplaces with sound levels averaging over 85 decibels for an eight-hour shift. While hobby woodworkers may not experience this noise level for that long, hearing damage is cumulative and irreversible, so protection is important. Standard earbuds offer little to no protection, but some have a decibel rating that meets OSHA standards. Disposable earplugs provide better protection, and earmuff-style hearing protection offers the highest level of safety.

Respiratory Protection

Wood dust is a known carcinogen, making respiratory protection important. Wearing a simple dust mask is certainly better than nothing, regardless of whether you have a full beard, stubble, or no facial hair. These straightforward tools serve as your shield against inhaling sawdust in your shop. By putting on a dust mask or respirator, you not only protect your lungs against potential harm, but also ensure that your love for woodworking remains a lifelong pursuit.

Small Part Safety

Toys often involve small parts, which can bring fingers close to blades and bits. To handle these small pieces safely, there are a few tricks you can use. One method is to create oversized pieces. For

The safest way to cut out pieces is to begin with oversized parts that you will later trim down to the appropriate size.

instance, when making the skid loader, cut the roof 3"–4" (76.2–101.6mm) longer than needed, profile both ends, and then cut the front from one end before trimming the roof to its final size.

Always keep the safety devices that come with tools in place; don't remove shrouds or guards. In this book, some devices were removed for clarity in images, but it's never advisable to do so. For safer cuts, make multiple pieces at once. For example, when making the flatbed truck bed, rip a 12" (305mm) piece, profile it, and then cut it to length for 2–3 trucks. Si milarly, make the biplane fuselage twice the final length, groove both sides, then cut to size. When using a router, work with the largest piece possible. Keep hands and fingers away from blades and bits at all times.

The scroll saw is your friend when it comes to cutting out small parts. It is one of the safest power

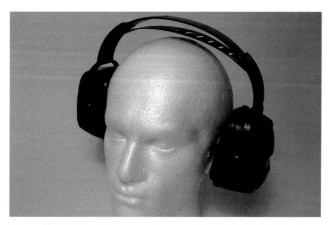

Earmuff-style hearing protection provides the highest level of protection.

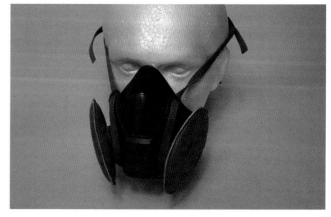

A dust mask or respirator is essential to protecting your lungs against harmful wood dust.

The safest and quickest way to profile multiple parts at once is to profile larger sections of wood and then cut them down to their final sizes.

tools in my shop. If I am concerned about the small size of a piece or tricky curves, I will cut it out on the scroll saw. This includes dowels and the exhaust on the jet. The scroll saw leaves a cleaner cut than the other saws, which makes it easier to sand.

Enhancing Tools

Consider investing in an adjustable aftermarket miter gauge or modify the one that came with your

Use or Donate Your Scraps

After each project, I usually end up with scrap blocks because I have oversized the blanks. This scrap is usually good lumber but too small to use or too small to keep. I gather these in a bucket, and I repurpose them into random-size blocks. Each one is belt-sanded to remove sharp edges. I either donate these blocks to a local group or post them on a local free site, ensuring that no leftover wood goes to waste.

saw by attaching a piece of wood to prevent twisting and binding during crosscuts, enhancing safety and precision. Safety tools are essential for toy-making. Aftermarket push sticks and pads, like a Grr-Ripper®-style push block, are helpful for ripping narrow pieces like bumpers and exhausts. Always use a push stick when the board is on the table saw to keep fingers safe. Push pads are useful for cutting grooves, rabbets, and for router work. Avoid using push blocks if the blade protrudes, unless designed for that purpose.

Child Safety

Children will be the primary users of these toys, and they will undoubtedly be the most severe critics. Kids tend to test the limits of toys, making safety a principal concern. Small parts that can be easily detached should be avoided at all costs, as they present a choking hazard if they come off or break.

Wheels and Pegs

Wheels and axle pegs are especially prone to coming loose with vigorous play. To address this issue, there are two effective methods. The first is to use pliers to crimp the ends of the pegs, providing more surface area for the glue to adhere to.

Alternatively, you can securely fasten the axle peg in the hole by pin-nailing it, which is the most reliable way to prevent the peg from coming loose and falling out. Be mindful of details like steering wheels, which can pose a choking hazard without adding significant value to the toy.

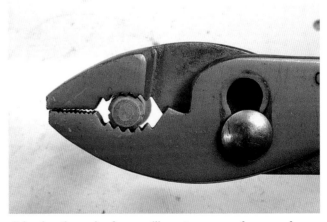

Crimping the ends of pegs will create more surface area for wood glue to adhere to, in turn making them less likely to slip out of a toy once the glue has cured.

Basic Techniques

The projects in this book require a few basic woodworking techniques. All are accessible to beginner woodworkers. In this section, we will cover those briefly, but more detailed instructions are available in the individual projects.

Wood Joints and Grain Direction

There are three main glue joints that are used in this book: wood to wood, dowel, and pegs. It is important to know how the pieces are being glued together. Plan the glue-up with the steps and clamps you will be using.

Wood to wood. Joining wood to wood involves connecting one piece of wood to another. This occurs when gluing an end or edge of a board to the face of another board or joining two edges together. It's crucial that the faces being glued are flat and free from visible gaps. Apply a bead of glue to the area being glued, spreading it evenly with a silicone brush or a scrap piece of wood for a consistent coat. The right amount of glue comes with practice.

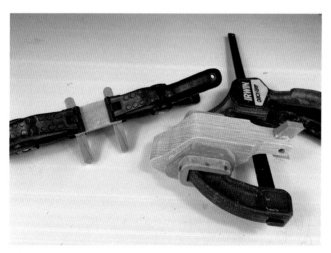

When you clamp wood pieces together, glue will likely squeeze out onto the workpiece. Wipe this away with a damp paper towel.

Gently push the pieces together and use clamps to hold them. Be cautious not to clamp too tightly. This can squeeze out all the glue, creating a weak joint. Any squeeze-out can be wiped away with a damp paper towel.

For complex glue-ups, like assembling tow truck and tractor cabs, perform a test fit first with all the clamps. This helps identify potential issues and ensures all necessary tools are within reach. Trying to hold pieces together while opening a clamp can be tricky, so proper preparation is important.

Dowel joints. These strengthen the bond of the pieces being joined and involve drilling a hole and inserting a dowel to reinforce a glue joint. For instance, in areas where there's limited surface area for a strong wood-to-wood bond, like the airfoil on the race car, dowel joints come in handy. They also enhance bonds between end grain and face grain, as demonstrated in the bumpers on the jeep and small truck. In specific cases, like the tow truck hook, a dowel is used to fortify a weak point prone to breakage.

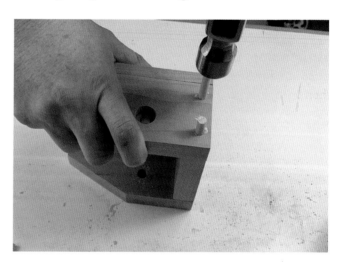

Adding dowels provides more stability in end-to-end or end-to-face joints, or when there isn't much surface area to provide a strong bond.

To create these joints, start by pre-drilling the face as a guide to drill the hole into the other piece. Glue the pieces together, and then drill the hole in the mating part to the appropriate depth. Then, cut a dowel slightly longer than the hole. Apply a bit of wood glue around the hole's sides and insert the dowel until it reaches the bottom. Once the glue has dried, trim any excess dowel and sand it smooth for a neat finish. These joints are not meant to move.

Peg joints are primarily used for affixing movable parts, such as wheels.

Peg joints. These are similar to dowel joints but with a couple of distinctions. They are specifically designed for movable parts such as wheels. In this case, premade or purchased pegs are used. Each part has two predrilled holes. The smaller hole requires glue, while the larger hole does not. This setup is commonly used for attaching wheels, like in the skid loader and tow truck, where pegs secure the arms to the truck. Apply glue to the stationary part, then assemble.

TIP

For many peg joints, it's essential to have some gap, allowing the moving part to freely move. Insert the peg until it feels right. While creating a fixture for wheels can optimize the gap, it's not always necessary. When working with kids, providing a folded business card with a notch cut out serves as a guide for the peg's depth. After a few wheels, they often get the hang of it and no longer need the guide.

Grain Direction and Strength

End grain is found on the cut ends of wood. Edge grain is found on the smooth sides. Face grain refers to the flat, wide surface of the board.

Understanding grain direction is crucial for ensuring the strength of your wooden toy. While some parts might not be strong on their own, assembling them with grain orientation in mind enhances overall strength. Let's define a couple of key terms.

End grain. This is the end part of the board resembling the trunk of a tree with partial rings. It excels in resisting compressive force without crushing, but lacks good bending strength.

Face grain and edge grain. We'll group these together. They represent the part of the board where the grain runs the board's length. Face grain offers excellent bending strength and some compressive strength.

Toy designs in this book carefully consider the strengths and weaknesses of wood. Although toys don't demand extensive structural support, they need to withstand impacts and play. The designs aim to optimize wood strength and use straightforward joinery for durable toys.

Understanding the best grain orientation for each part is vital. For instance, the tow truck cab sides benefit from horizontal grain, providing resistance to breaking, especially around a window cutout. The addition of a back piece enhances overall strength. On the contrary, the tractor, with a large side cutout and no back panel, features vertical grain for increased strength.

In the case of the garbage truck, the lift arms use a unique strengthening method. Grooves are cut in the sides of the arms for thin strips to be added. While the arms have vertical grain, the strips are horizontal. This adds strength because of the cross grain.

Batch Production

Batch production allows for efficient creation of multiple handmade toys by reducing machine setups. Key elements include planning, setup, and consistency. Start by determining the quantity of each toy to produce. Use spreadsheets to list toy names, parts, dimensions, thicknesses, and purchased parts for better organization. This helps create a cut list, optimize operations, and streamline lumber buying. A bill of materials in a spreadsheet can calculate lumber needs by multiplying length by quantity and adding 15–25% for scrap. Sorting by width helps cut similar pieces in succession for efficiency.

Setup

A reliable setup is crucial for consistent results when producing a large batch of toys. Ensure uniformity in part sizes and hole placements to simplify the building process. Three critical areas for a robust setup are transferring the patterns, cutting, and drilling.

Transferring Patterns

When making multiple copies of a toy, I use a sturdy template made from ⅛" (3mm) hardboard. This allows me to create one pattern and use it repeatedly. Drill ⅛" (3mm) holes at hole locations for easy marking on the blank with an awl, and note the hole diameters on the template. Cut the template on a scroll saw and use it to transfer the pattern, saving paper, tape, and time.

Cutting

For cutting blanks to the same size, use a table saw or miter saw with a secured fence or stop block. Avoid applying too much force to prevent shifting. Maintain consistent grooves/rabbets with a stable fence and steady downward pressure.

Drilling

Precise and consistent hole drilling is vital, especially for wheel placement. Create a fence and stops to accurately locate and keep the holes perpendicular to the part. A simple block of wood clamped to the drill press table can serve as an effective setup. Use the same setup to ensure matching parts, such as holes in the roof and sides of certain toy models.

I don't use the drill press for assembly holes; instead, I use my cordless drill. I guide the bit through the existing hole to ensure accuracy. To maintain consistent hole depth, I wrap four or five layers of tape around the bit, folding the end over to create a tab that clears dust when the depth is reached. This method also helps measure the dowel length needed to fill the hole.

I do not have a fancy fence on my drill press. I have a block of 2" (51mm) thick board that is about 12" (305mm) long. I clamp this to the table as a fence. I have made grooved pieces that will rest on top of the block and slightly above the table to act as stops.

Dust can hinder accurate placement of parts against fences and stop blocks, particularly on the drill press, which lacks an effective dust collection system. I place a ⅛" (3mm) piece under the fence and stop to create a dust channel, keeping the surfaces clear. If needed,

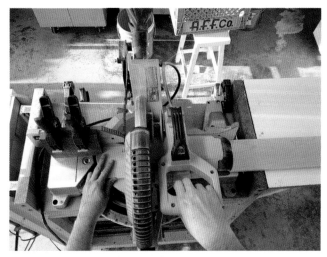

A miter saw is an excellent tool to consistently cut blanks to the same size. It's also useful for angled cuts.

To ensure you drill holes to a consistent depth, you can use tape to make a jig, of sorts.

A simple block of wood will make a sufficient stop for your drill press drill bit.

A thin piece of wood under a drill press fence and stop can create a channel to make dust collection easier.

I use a small shop vacuum to clean out the channels, helping maintain consistency when making multiple copies of the same toy.

Consistency

Consistency in material and blank sizes is critical, whether producing one toy or a batch. Varying thicknesses, even by less than 1⁄16" (1.6mm), can significantly impact dimensions. Obtain lumber from the same source or plane the material at the same time for uniformity.

Guard against dust accumulation. Dust and wood chips will cause parts to be inconsistent from one piece to another and one hole to another. Regularly clean the workspace. Elevate stop blocks slightly to allow dust to pass underneath, and secure setups to prevent movement during use.

Batching out toys is an efficient way to produce a large quantity while minimizing time spent on setups. It ensures uniformity, precision, and effective use of resources throughout the production process.

Introduction to Band Saws

A band saw is a versatile tool in woodworking, especially useful for toy makers for its ability to make precise cuts quickly, from simple blocks to complex shapes. The saw operates with a continuous loop blade that accommodates both straight and intricate curved cuts, ideal for handling multiple projects simultaneously through stack cutting.

ANATOMY OF A BAND SAW

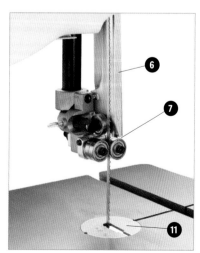

1. **Wheel cover**
   Protects operator from wheel and blade; may be removable or hinged to provide access to wheel.

2. **Wheel**
   Rimmed by a rubber tire that cushions the blade and keeps it from slipping.

3. **Throat column**
   Supports blade between wheels and protects oper-ator from blade.

4. **Table lock knob**
   Allows table to be tilted for bevel or compound cuts; a second knob is located on opposite side of table.

5. **Tension handle**
   Raises and lowers upper wheel to adjust blade tension.

6. **Blade guard**
   Protects operator from blade; moved up and down with guide assembly.

7. **Upper guide assembly**
   Raised and lowered depending on thickness of workpiece; includes blade guard, thrust bearing and guide blocks. Setscrews release guide blocks for lateral adjustment; thumbscrews release bearing and blocks for front-to-back adjustment by means of adjusting knobs. (A fixed guide assembly with thrust bearing and guide blocks is located under table insert.)

8. **Miter gauge**
   Guides workpiece across table for crosscuts or miter cuts.

9. **Rip fence**
   Guides workpiece across table for rip cuts, crosscuts and resawing.

10. **Table leveling pin**
    Adjustable to keep miter gauge slot properly aligned.

11. **Table insert**
    Prevents wood pieces from falling into table and supports workpiece when close to blade; usually made of aluminum.

12. **Dust spout**
    For dust collection system.

13. **On/Off switch**
    Can be padlocked in off position for safety.

Using a Band Saw to Cut Interior Spaces

Although a scroll saw or jig saw are the recommended tools of choice when making detailed interior cuts, a band saw can get the job done following the below steps.

- **Recommended Blade:** ¼" or ⅛" (3 or 6mm) width
- **TPI:** 10 or higher
- **Blade Thickness:** .025" or thinner

Note: ⅛" band saw blades are considered a specialty blade and will most likely not be available at larger chain stores. Specialty retailers who focus on providing a full range of woodworking tools and supplies will keep a stock of specialty blades on hand for most standard sized saws. They are readily available for online purchase.

1. After the pattern has been drawn and exterior cuts have been made, make one crosscut through the side to the center of the interior, following the wood grain. Cutting across the grain will make the cut more challenging to hide when glued back together. Make the cut through the middle of a side, not through a corner or intricate detail that will be altered by the cut of the blade.

2. Cut straight to the center of the interior space, then back up within the interior area. Make a second curved cut to the end of the first cut. These two cuts will create an opening for the blade to turn more easily, minimizing stress on the wood and blade.

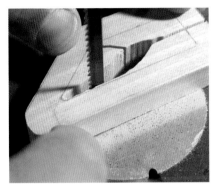

3. Cut a straight relief cut to each corner. Go back to the center and make gentle curved cuts to the middle of each side, cutting to the corner.

4. Repeat the process with each side until the interior area has been removed.

5. After the interior has been removed, work a strong bond wood glue into the open side cut. For small pieces, use a toothpick to work the glue in from all sides versus trying to pry the sides apart, which may result in the piece snapping in two.

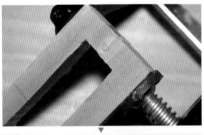

6. Clamp and allow the piece to dry per the recommended manufacturer's instructions. After the glue has dried, sand and finish. As shown, the side cut will no longer be visible.

Introduction to Scroll Saws

A scroll saw is an electrically powered saw with a reciprocating blade that moves up and down to cut through wood and other materials. One of the main advantages of a scroll saw is its removable blade, which you can easily insert into a predrilled hole and cut outward from the center of your project. Thanks to the scroll saw's versatility and ability to handle curves, tight corners, and tricky cuts, it is an excellent choice for intricate projects. Since the blade and saw are fixed, your job is to move the workpiece around, rather than moving the tool in relation to the workpiece. Remember to go slow, and let the blade do the work.

Scroll Saw Basics

A scroll saw operates with a short, fine blade that moves up and down at high speed. This tool is ideal for creating precise cuts and detailed patterns in thin wood, which is often required in toy making:

- **Blade selection:** Choosing the right blade is crucial for achieving the desired outcome. Blades vary in tooth design, size, and material, each suited for different types of cuts and materials. For intricate work in toy making, finer blades with more teeth per inch are preferred.

- **Speed control:** Most scroll saws offer variable speed settings, which can be adjusted based on the complexity of the cut and the type of material being used. Slower speeds are typically used for intricate cuts to ensure control and accuracy.

Cutting with Scroll Saws

Scroll saws excel at fine work and can be used to enhance the detail and precision of toy parts:

- **Intricate cuts:** The scroll saw's ability to make very tight turns and intricate cuts makes it perfect for the toys in this book. This capability allows toy makers to create complex shapes and small pieces that would be difficult to achieve with other saws.

- **Piercing cuts:** One of the unique features of a scroll saw is its ability to make interior cuts without an entry slot. This is done by threading the blade through a predrilled hole in the workpiece, which allows for complex interior cutouts without affecting the exterior of the piece.

- **Stack cutting:** Similar to band saws, scroll saws can be used for stack cutting, but typically with thinner materials. This method allows for multiple copies of a piece to be cut simultaneously, which is useful for mass production of small, detailed toy parts.

- **Pattern work:** Scroll saws are particularly well-suited for following pattern lines closely. Using temporary adhesives to attach paper patterns directly to the wood can streamline the cutting process, ensuring high fidelity to the original design.

Scroll saw blades come in a variety of sizes and profiles. For the purposes of these projects, #5 and #7 skip-tooth blades are your best bet. For more on blade size selection, see the table on page 29.

ANATOMY OF A SCROLL SAW

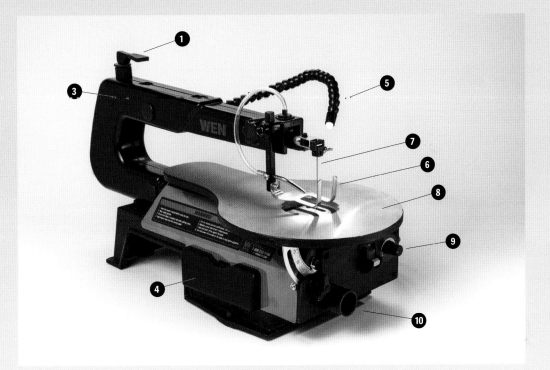

1. **Tension knob**
   This allows the user to adjust the blade's tension to preferred specifications. One must relieve blade tension to change out blades, as well.

2. **Blower nozzle**
   This helps to blow sawdust off your workpiece as you cut, essential for keeping pattern and cut lines clear so you can follow them.

3. **Base/arm**
   This houses tensioners and various components necessary to operation.

4. **Blade storage**
   Not all scroll saws will have this feature, but it's handy to keep blade replacements nearby.

5. **Work light**
   One can never have enough light in the workshop.

6. **Footer**
   This applies pressure to the workpiece and helps with stability. It also acts as a guard to protect the user from accidents.

7. **Blade**
   See the table below for more information on blade selection.

8. **Worktable**
   This is where your workpiece will rest as you cut out parts.

9. **Speed control**
   This allows you to adjust the cutting speed to suit your needs.

10. **Dust port**
    This allows you to hook up a shop vac or dust collection system to help mitigate sawdust in the workshop.

MATCHING WOOD TO BLADES

Wood	Thickness	Blade Size
Hardwood, softwood, plywood	1/4" (6mm) or thinner	#2/0 to #1
Hardwood, softwood, plywood	1/4" (6mm) to 1/2" (1.3cm)	#1 to #2
Hardwood, softwood, plywood	1/2" (1.3cm) to 3/4" (1.9cm)	#3 to #4
Hardwood (less dense), softwood, plywood	3/4" (1.9cm) to 1" (2.5cm)	#4 to #6
Hardwood (dense)	3/4" (1.9cm) to 1" (2.5cm)	#5 to #7

Projects

TUGBOAT

Patterns on pages 102–103

Who doesn't love a tugboat, the small but crucial vessel that moves larger ships through a harbor? This project's compact size makes it a simple toy children can play with on any surface. It even floats! I've also built in a number of details for little hands to grasp.

TOOLS & MATERIALS

- Scroll saw blades: #5 skip-tooth
- Drill press with bits: ¼" (6mm), ¹¹⁄₃₂" (9mm), ⅝" (16mm), ¾" (19mm) dia.
- Router with roundover bit: ⅛" (3mm) radius
- Sander: random orbit
- Sandpaper: 220 grit
- Small clamps
- Wood glue
- Blue painter's tape
- Finish: clear shellac (or other child-safe finish)
- Spray adhesive

Woods (see Parts List for exact dimensions)

- Deck and roof: cherry, ⅜" (9mm) thick
- Hull, cabin, and lower cabin: maple, ¾" (18mm) thick
- Wooden dowel, ¼" (6mm)-dia.
- Smokestack: walnut dowel, ¾" (18mm)-dia.
- Wooden axle peg: ¹¹⁄₃₂" (9mm) dia.

PARTS LIST: TUGBOAT

	Part	Quantity	Materials	Dimensions
A	Deck	1	Cherry, ⅜" (9mm) thick	3 ¼" x 7" (8.3 x 17.8cm)
B	Hull	1	Maple, ¾" (18mm) thick	2 ¾" x 6 ½" (7 x 16.5cm)
C	Cabin	1	Maple, ¾" (18mm) thick	1 ¼" x 1 ½" (3.2 x 3.8cm)
D	Roof	1	Cherry, ⅜" (9mm) thick	1 ¾" x 2" (4.4 x 5.1cm)
E	Lower cabin	1	Maple, ¾" (18mm) thick	1 ¼" x 3 ½" (3.2 x 8.9cm)
F	Smokestack	1	Walnut dowel, ¾" (18mm)-dia.	1 ½" (3.8cm) long
G	Assembly dowels	5	¼" (6mm)-dia.	6" (15.2cm) long
H	Axle peg	1	¹¹⁄₃₂" (9mm) dia.	1 1/4" (30mm) long

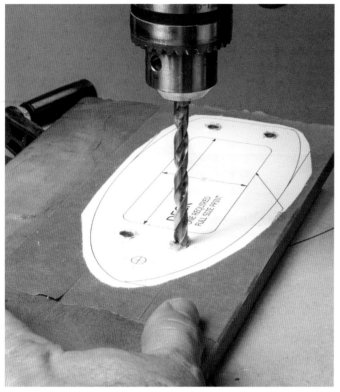

1 **Attach the hull and deck patterns to the wood blanks.** Use spray adhesive. Drill ¼" (6mm) holes in the areas indicated on the deck pattern. Then, cut out the pieces. Sand the edges smooth with 220-grit sandpaper in a belt sander, and set aside the inside deck cutout. You'll use this piece to make the roof. Cut the lower cabin, cabin, and roof pieces. Glue and clamp the upper and lower cabin pieces together and let dry.

2 **Mark and drill the window and smokestack holes.** I used a ⅝" (16mm)-dia. bit for the window and a ¾" (19mm)-dia. bit for the smokestack. Mark and establish the curve on the front of the cabin using a belt sander.

3 **Glue and clamp the roof on the cabin assembly.** Let dry. Then, mark and drill an ¹¹⁄₃₂" (9mm)-dia. hole on the roof for the axle peg.

TIP

Be careful to not drill the assembly dowel holes all the way through the hull. This will prevent blowout on the back side.

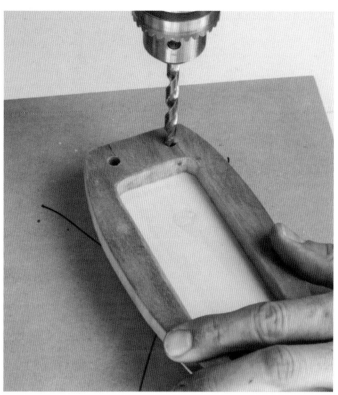

4 **Round the hull, deck, and roof.** Use a ⅛" (3mm)-radius roundover bit in a router.

5 **Glue the deck to the hull.** Drill ¼" (6mm)-dia. by 1" (2.5cm) deep holes in the deck. Cut a ¼" (6mm)-dia. dowel to 1⅛" (2.9cm) long. Then, glue the dowel pieces in and sand smooth. Sand all parts to 220-grit. Glue in the smokestack and axle peg.

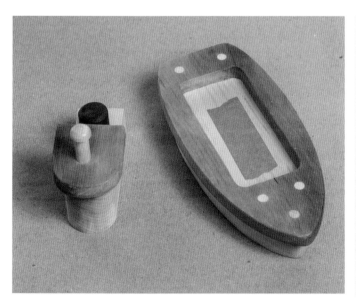

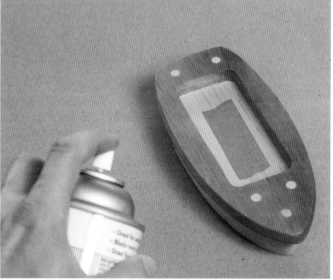

6 **Finish the pieces.** Cover the center of the deck cutout with blue painter's tape. If you leave this area uncovered, the lacquer will interfere with the adhesive. Finish the pieces with shellac or another clear, child-safe finish. Buff lightly with 220-grit sandpaper and apply a second coat of finish. Remove the tape, and glue the cabin and deck assemblies together with wood glue.

CITY CARS

Patterns on pages 104–107

This is a quick project with many finishing possibilities. Cut them out of attractive hardwoods or decorate them with bright acrylic paints. The cars are sturdy and have plenty of places for little fingers to grab and hold onto. This project is also great for showing the young woodworker in your life how to use a scroll saw and a drill press. Start your engines and see where your creativity takes you!

A youth group requested these designs for older children. Their members wanted simple and easy to make toys for donation to a local charity. Kids like to paint them, and they feel they've helped make them by putting on the wheels.

TOOLS & MATERIALS

- Scroll saw with #5 and #9 skip-tooth blades
- Belt or disc sander
- Drill press with 5⁄16" (8mm)-dia. bit
- Clamps
- Paintbrushes (optional)
- Spray adhesive
- Blue painter's tape
- Sandpaper: 100, 150, and 220 grit
- Wood glue
- Food-safe finish, such as shellac or beeswax and walnut oil
- Acrylic paints (optional)

Woods (see Parts List for exact dimensions)

- Bug body: poplar, 1 ½" (3.8cm) thick
- Bug fenders: cherry, ⅜" (9mm) thick
- Mini body: maple, 1 ¼" (30mm) thick
- Mini fenders (two each): walnut, ⅜" (9mm) thick
- Sedan fenders (two each): walnut, ½" (12mm) thick
- Sedan body and sports car: oak, 1¼" (30mm) thick
- Sports car fenders: cherry, ½" (12mm) thick
- Wooden dowels: ¼" (6mm)-dia.
- Wooden treaded wheels: 1¼" (30mm)-dia.

PARTS LIST: CITY CARS

	Part	Quantity (per car)	Materials	Dimensions
A	Mini body	1	Maple, 1 ¼" (30mm) thick	3 ¼" x 5" (8.3 x 12.7cm)
B	Mini fenders	2	Walnut, ⅜" (9mm) thick	1 ⅝" x 5" (4.1 x 12.7cm)
C	Sports car body	1	Oak, 1 ¼" (30mm) thick	3 ¼" 6 ¾" (8.3 x 17.2cm)
D	Sports car fenders	2	Cherry, ½" (12mm) thick	1 ¼" x 6 ¾" (3.2 x 17.2cm)
E	Bug body	1	Maple, 1 ¼" (30mm) thick	3 ¼" x 5 ¾" (8.3 x 14.6cm)
F	Bug fenders	2	Oak, ⅜" (9mm) thick	1 ⅜" x 5 ¾" (3.5 x 14.6cm)
G	Sedan body	1	Oak, 1 ¼" (30mm) thick	3 ¼" x 7 ¼" (8.3 x 18.4cm)
H	Sedan fenders	2	Oak, ⅜" (9mm) thick	1 ¾" x 7 ¼" (4.4 x 18.4cm)
I	Wheels, treaded	16	1 ¼" (30mm)-dia., purchased	⅜" (9mm) thick
J	Assembly dowels	8	¼" (6mm)-dia.	1 ¾" (4.4cm) long

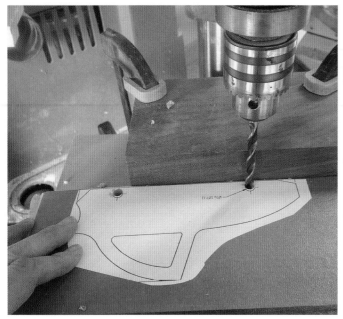

1 **Prepare the blanks and drill entry holes.** For these, make oversized blanks of 1½" (3. 8cm) material for the car bodies and ½" (1. 3cm) material for the fenders. Cover one face with painter's tape. Cut out the patterns and use spray adhesive to attach each pattern to the blank. Then, drill 9/16" (8mm) holes in the bodies for wheel axles. You can use the same bit to drill blade entry holes in the windows.

2 **Use a #9 skip-tooth blade to cut out the bodies.** Go slow and steady. If you push the blade, it tends to bend and not cut the wood straight up and down. This may cause the blade to bind and break. Cut out the windows.

3 **Use a #5 skip-tooth blade to cut out the fenders.** While not necessary, I like to use a router to create a 1/8" (3mm) radius on one side of the fenders and the window.

4 Sand all parts using 100- and 150-grit sandpaper. Use the wheels as guides to glue the fenders on the body of the car. Clamp and let the glue dry.

5 Sand the fenders flush with the body. For this, I use a belt sander. Then cut the dowel for the axles. The length of the axle will depend on the wheel you use. You should have a ⅛" (3mm) total gap between the wheels and body. Glue one wheel on each axle. Put the axle through the 9/16" (8mm) hole in the body.

6 Apply a child-safe finish. I used shellac. Once dry, glue the second wheel of each pair into place.

FIGHTER JET

Patterns on page 108

With a simple construction and no moving parts, this fighter jet is a great way to dip your toes into toy making. Cut the fuselage shape, glue on some wings, and presto—you have an instant classic that kids will love!

TOOLS & MATERIALS

- Scroll saw with blades: #5 reverse-tooth and #7 skip-tooth
- Drill press with ⅝" (16mm) Forstner bit
- Sanders: belt, disc (optional)
- Vise
- Clamps
- Table saw (optional)
- Spray adhesive
- Wood glue
- Clear packaging tape

- Sandpaper: assorted grits to 320
- Finish, such as clear shellac
- Acrylic paints (optional)

Woods (see Parts List for exact dimensions)

- Exhaust, rudder, wings: cherry, ⁵⁄₁₆" (8mm) thick
- Fuselage: oak, ¾" (18mm) thick

PARTS LIST: FIGHTER JET

	Part	Quantity	Materials	Dimensions
A	Exhaust	4	Cherry, ⁵⁄₁₆" (8mm) thick	⁵⁄₁₆" x 3 ½" (8mm x 8.9cm)
B	Rudder	2	Cherry, ⁵⁄₁₆" (8mm) thick	1" (25mm) square
C	Wings	2	Cherry, ⁵⁄₁₆" (8mm) thick	2 ⅛" x 3 ½" (5.4 x 8.9cm)
D	Fuselage	1	Oak, ¾" (18mm) thick	1 ½" x 5" (3.8 x 12.7cm)

1 **Cut the fuselage blank.** It should be 1¾" x 5½" (45 x 140mm). Trace or adhere the pattern to the blank with the back bottom corner lined up with the back and bottom of the blank. Mark the hole of the engine on the end of the blank and use a ⅝" (16mm) Forstner bit to drill a flat bottom hole ¼" (6mm) deep. Use a #7 skip-tooth blade to cut the fuselage body out. Set aside until the wing assemblies are complete.

2 **Sand the nose of the fighter.** Use a belt sander or palm sander. You can also use a scroll saw to cut away the bulk of the material before sanding. At this point, start with 100-grit sandpaper to sand all the pieces and round over any sharp edges. Finish with 150-grit sandpaper.

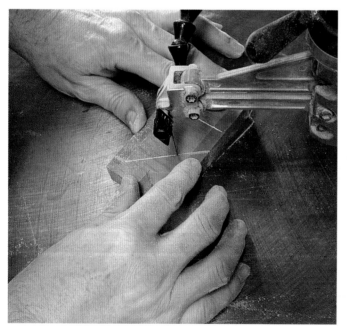

3 **Cut the blanks out for each of the wings and rudders.** Trace or adhere the pattern to the blanks. I like to tape the wing blanks together so I can cut both wings out at the same time. Cut the wings and rudders out using a #7 skip-tooth blade.

4 **Use a push block to rip the exhaust pieces to width on a table saw or band saw.** Cut them to length using a scroll saw or handsaw. The 45-degree bevel can also be cut with a saw or it can be sanded.

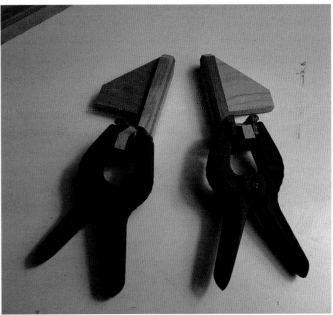

5 Glue the exhaust pieces to the wings. Use spring clamps to keep the pieces in place while the glue dries. After the glue dries, remove any squeeze-out and sand the exhaust pieces flush to the wing.

6 Glue the rudders to the tops of the wings and exhaust. It is easier to do this step before the wings are attached to the fuselage because a spring clamp can be used to hold them in place.

7 Glue the wing assemblies to the fuselage. Clamp the parts together using spring clamps on the exhaust pieces or quick grip clamps on the wings. Clean up any glue squeeze-out. Finish using a child-safe finish or leave it unfinished.

MODEL T

Patterns on pages 110–111

Making toys for children has always made me happy. I gravitate toward making designs inspired by iconic vehicles—and what's more iconic than the Model T? This project is small enough to be made from offcuts and can be enjoyed by all ages.

Get creative and paint your finished piece or use contrasting hardwoods to showcase the car's different components.

TOOLS & MATERIALS

- Scroll saw with #5 skip-tooth blade
- Drill with bits: ¼" (6mm); ⁷⁄₃₂" (5.6mm) brad point
- Belt sander
- Hammer
- Ruler
- Clamps
- Awl
- Table saw (optional)
- Wood glue
- Spray adhesive
- Blue painter's tape (optional)
- Sandpaper: assorted grits 100 to 150
- Clean cloth
- White colored pencil (optional)
- Clear nontoxic finish, such as shellac

Woods (see Parts List for exact dimensions)

- Chassis, back and sides: cherry, ¾" (18mm) thick
- Engine: cherry, 1" (3.8cm) thick
- Roof and fender: oak, ½" (12mm) thick
- Back assembly: wooden dowels, ³⁄₁₆" (5.6mm)-dia.
- Front assembly: wooden dowels, ¼" (6mm)-dia.
- Wooden axle pegs: ⁷⁄₃₂" (5.6mm)-dia.
- Treaded wooden wheels: 1½" (30mm)-dia.

PARTS LIST: MODEL T

	Part	Quantity	Materials	Dimensions
A	Chassis	1	Cherry, ¾" (18mm) thick	2 ¼" x 3" (5.7 x 7.6cm)
B	Back	1	Cherry, ¾" (18mm) thick	1" x 1 ¼" (2.5 x 3.2cm)
C	Car sides	2	Cherry, ¾" (18mm) thick	2 ¼" x 2 ½" (5.7 x 6.4cm)
D	Roof	1	Oak, ½" (12mm) thick	2 ¼" x 2 ¾" (5.7 x 7cm)
E	Fender	1	Oak, ½" (12mm) thick	1 ¼" x 3 ⅞" (3.2 x 9.8cm)
F	Engine	1	Cherry, 1" (25mm) thick	1 ¼" x 2 ¼" (23.2 x 3.2cm)
G	Axle pegs	4	⁷⁄₃₂" (5.6mm)-dia.	1 ⅛" (2.9cm) long
H	Back assembly dowels	2	³⁄₁₆" (5mm)-dia.	1 ¼" (30mm) long
I	Front assembly dowels	2	¼" (6mm)-dia.	2" (5.1cm) long
J	Wheels, treaded	4	1 ½" (3.8cm)-dia., purchased	½" (12mm) thick

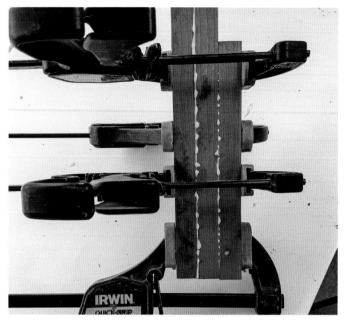

1 **Transfer the patterns to the blanks and cut the pieces.** For the engine, I glued up three smaller pieces of scrap wood to form a larger piece, but you can cut it on a scroll saw or band using a single piece of wood.

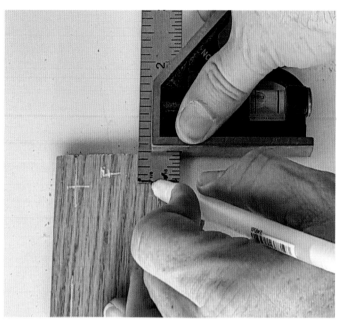

2 **Mark the roof.** Using a white pencil, mark the front of the roof and all four hole locations for the dowels. *Note: The front holes are in a slightly different location than the back holes.*

3 **Drill the holes in the car sides and roof.** Set up a guide block to ensure the holes are drilled at the same offset from the edge. Drill ¼" (6mm) and ³⁄₁₆" (5mm) through-holes at the marked locations on the roof. Drill the ¼" (6mm) holes in the front of the car sides, 1½" (3. 8cm) deep, using a brad point drill bit. Then, change the setup to correct the offset for the chassis. Drill ⁷⁄₃₂" (5. 6mm) holes in the chassis for the axle pegs.

4 **Assemble the car body.** Glue the sides and middle together. Make sure the backs and bottoms are flush with each other. Clamp the assembly and let dry.

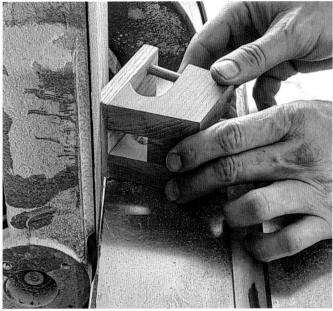

5 **Attach the roof.** Put the roof on, and then push it down until the back sits flush with the sides. Insert the ³⁄₁₆" (5mm) and ¼" (6mm)-dia. dowels into their respective holes, hammer them in place, and then secure with wood glue, wiping off squeeze-out.

6 **Shape the roof.** Mark the side profile on the roof. Use the belt sander with 100-grit sandpaper to profile it. Sand all other parts smooth and flush.

7 **Assemble the car.** Glue the side assembly and the engine to the chassis. Clamp the three pieces together, wipe off squeeze-out, and let dry. Hand-sand the assembly and fenders smooth, moving progressively through the grits from 100 to 150.

8 **Attach the fenders.** Test-fit the wheels to see where the fenders should sit. I left about ⅛" (3mm) margin between the fender and wheel so that the wheel could rotate freely. Glue and clamp the fender onto the car, removing squeeze-out. Let dry.

9 **Add finishing touches.** Sand the entire project to 150 grit. Finish with a nontoxic finish, such as shellac, or leave the project natural. Attach the wheels with axle pegs and seat them with a hammer.

JEEP

Patterns on pages 112–113

A Jeep can go just about anywhere. They can cruise through the city, handle rocky terrain, or tackle dunes at the beach. My version is a great toy for a child and a fun gift for a Jeep lover.

I like this design for two main reasons: it is small enough to be made from scrap lumber, and you can make several in a sitting. The toy vehicle is assembled with glue and dowels, so it's sure to handle rough play and come out on top.

TOOLS & MATERIALS

- Scroll saw with #5 skip-tooth blade
- Drill with bits: ³⁄₁₆" (5mm), ⁷⁄₃₂" (5.6mm), ½" (13mm)-dia.
- Belt sander
- Hammer
- Clamps
- Awl
- Wood glue
- Spray adhesive
- Sandpaper: assorted grits to 320
- Clean cloth
- Child-safe finish, such as clear shellac

Woods (see Parts List for exact dimensions)

- Fenders: cherry, ½" (12mm) thick
- Chassis, engine center, engine left, engine right, and back sides: walnut, ¾" (18mm) thick
- Bumpers and back center, cherry, ¾" (18mm) thick
- Top bar: cherry, ⅜" (9mm) thick
- Wooden dowel, ³⁄₁₆" (5mm)-dia.
- Wooden axle pegs: ⁷⁄₃₂" (5.6mm)-dia.
- Treaded wooden wheels: 1½" (3.8cm)-dia.

PARTS LIST: JEEP

	Part	Quantity	Materials	Dimensions
A	Fenders	2	Cherry, ½" (12mm) thick	1" x 4 ⅜" (2.5 x 11.1cm)
B	Chassis	1	Walnut, ¾" (18mm) thick	2 ¼" x 4" (5.7 x 10.2cm)
C	Engine center	1	Walnut, ¾" (18mm) thick	⅞" x 2" (2.2 x 5.1cm)
D	Engine Left	1	Walnut, ¾" (18mm) thick	⅞" x 1 ½" (2.2 x 3.8cm)
E	Engine right	1	Walnut, ¾" (18mm) thick	⅞" x 1 ½" (2.2 x 3.8cm)
F	Back sides	2	Walnut, ¾" (18mm) thick	1 ⅝" x 2 ½" (4.1 x 6.4cm)
G	Axle pegs	4	⁷⁄₃₂" (5.6mm)-dia., purchased	1 ½" (3.8cm) long
H	Bumpers	2	Cherry, ¾" (18mm) thick	⅜" x 3 ¼" (1 x 8.3cm)
I	Wheels, treaded	4	1 ½" (3.8cm)-dia., purchased	½" (12mm) thick
J	Back center	1	Cherry, ¾" (18mm) thick	⅞" x ¾" (2.2 x 1.9cm)
K	Assembly dowels	6	³⁄₁₆" (5mm)-dia., purchased	1 ¼" (30mm) long
L	Top bar	1	Cherry, ⅜" (9mm) thick	½" x 2 ¼" (1.3 x 5.7cm)

1 **Transfer the patterns to the blanks and cut them out.** You can affix the patterns to the blanks or draw them directly on. Cut all parts on a scroll saw.

2 **Mark the holes for the wheels on the sides of the chassis.** Drill a 1" (25mm)-deep hole in each location with a ⁷⁄₃₂" (5.6mm)-dia. bit in a drill press. Then, mark the holes for the headlights on the front of each side piece. Using clamps and a support block for stability, drill ¼" (6mm)-deep holes in each location with a ½" (12mm)-dia. bit in the drill press.

3 **Assemble the Jeep body.** Glue and clamps parts E and F together. Then, glue and clamp parts C and D together. Do not glue the two units together, but make sure the front and back side pieces sit on the same plane. Let dry.

4 **Shape the pieces.** Use a belt sander to sand the sides of the glue-ups from Step 3. Remove the dust with a clean cloth, and then glue the units together. Once dry, glue the Jeep body to the chassis, and then sand the sides and chassis flush.

5 **Mark the holes for the top bar and bumpers.** Glue and clamp the pieces in place. When dry, drill ³⁄₁₆" (5mm)-dia. holes, about 1" (2. 5cm) deep, in the locations specified on the patterns. Then, cut six 1" (2. 5cm)-long pieces from a ³⁄₁₆" (5mm)-dia. dowel. Glue the dowels into the holes. Sand the dowels flush with the assembly.

6 **Add the fenders and wheels.** Use axle pegs to dry-fit the wheels before gluing on the fenders. You want to make sure that the wheels have enough space to spin freely once attached. Once you are satisfied, glue and clamp the pieces in place and remove any squeeze-out. Once dry, hand-sand all surfaces with 150-grit sandpaper.

7 **Finish using a child-safe finish or leave the surface natural.** Cut the axle pegs down to size, if necessary, and use a hammer to seat the wheels.

RACE CAR

Patterns on page 109

Nothing beats the thrill of racing around corners at top speeds, trying to pass or outmaneuver other drivers. Whether down a ramp or flat on the ground, this toy is great for speeding around the racetrack toward that famous checkered flag. I made this design so kids could paint their own cars and then attach the wheels to race. You can build just one or enough for every kid on the block.

TOOLS & MATERIALS

- Scroll saw with #5 skip-tooth blade
- Drill press with bits: ³⁄₁₆" (5mm)-dia., ⁷⁄₃₂" (5.6mm)-dia.
- Router with ¼" (6mm)-dia. roundover bit (optional)
- Sanders: belt, pneumatic drum
- Hammer
- Clamps
- Awl
- White colored pencil
- Wood glue
- Spray adhesive
- Sandpaper: assorted grits up to 320

- Child-safe finish, such as clear shellac

Woods (see Parts List for exact dimensions)

- Side appliques: walnut, ½" (12mm) thick
- Center section and sides: walnut or cherry, ¾" (18mm) thick
- Tail wing: cherry, ⅜" (9mm) thick
- Wooden dowel, ³⁄₁₆" (5mm)-dia.
- Wooden axle pegs: ⁷⁄₃₂" (5.6mm)-dia.
- Treaded wooden wheels: 4

PARTS LIST: RACE CAR

	Part	Quantity	Materials	Dimensions
A	Side appliqués	2	Walnut, ½" (12mm) thick	⅝" x 1 ¼" (1.6 x 3.2cm)
B	Sides	2	Walnut/Cherry, ¾" (18mm) thick	⅞" x 4 ¼" (2.2 x 10.8cm)
C	Center section	1	Walnut/Cherry, ¾" (18mm) thick	1 ½" x 4 ¾" (3.8 x 12.1cm)
D	Tail wing	1	Cherry, ⅜" (9mm) thick	⅞" x 3 ½" (2.2 x 8.9cm)
	Wooden dowel	1	³⁄₁₆" (5mm)-dia.	3" (7.6cm) long
E	Back wheels, treaded	2	1 ½" (30mm)-dia., purchased	½" (1.3cm) thick
F	Front wheels, treaded	2	1 ¼" (30mm)-dia., purchased	½" (1.3cm) thick
G	Axle pegs	4	⁷⁄₃₂" (5.6mm)-dia.	1 ⅛" (2.9cm) long

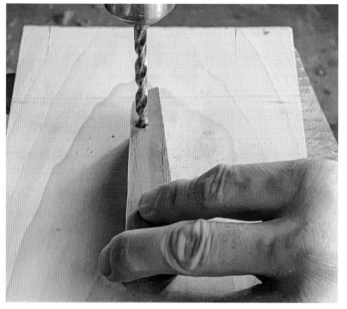

1 **Transfer the patterns to the blank.** You can affix the patterns to the wood or draw them on directly. Cut all parts on a scroll saw or band saw.

2 **Mark the holes for the wheels on the side body pieces.** Drill a hole in each location with a ⁷⁄₃₂" (5.6mm)-dia. drill bit in a drill press.

For a Different Look

Round over the top of the appliques with a router or a pneumatic drum sander and sand a bevel on the wing for a softer look.

3 Glue and clamp the three body pieces together. Once dry, sand the bottom and back flush using a belt sander. Round all sharp edges and corners with 150-grit sandpaper.

4 Cut the tail wing to size. Mark two ³⁄₁₆" (5mm) holes in the center of the wing, where it will sit on the body of the car. Then, glue and clamp the wing to the back of the race car assembly. Drill the holes in the marked areas. I do this by wrapping blue painter's tape around the bit about ⁵⁄₈" (1. 6cm) up from the tip. This is so I don't drill down farther than necessary. Cut the dowels to size and insert them into the holes with a hammer, sanding until they are flush with the surface.

5 Temporarily attach the wheels. This will give you a sense of where to place the appliques. Glue and clamp the appliques to the sides. Remove the wheels and sand all surfaces with 150-grit sandpaper. Sand progressively up through the grits until you reach 320.

6 Finish using a child-safe finish or leave the surface natural. Attach the wheels with axle pegs, cutting them down to size if necessary.

FLATBED TRUCK

Patterns on pages 114–115

The flatbed truck is designed for hauling, and its toughness extends from transporting cars to furniture. I value its versatility and it makes a good toy to haul items from one imaginative area to another. I enjoy seeing the items that kids will haul on the flatbed.

TOOLS & MATERIALS

- Scroll saw with #5 and #7 skip-tooth blades
- Drill press with bits: 3⁄16" (4mm), 7⁄32" (5mm), 1⁄4" (6mm)-dia.
- Belt or disc sander (optional)
- Clamps
- Table saw (optional)
- Clear packaging tape
- Spray adhesive
- Wood glue
- Sandpaper: assorted grits to 220
- Finish, such as clear shellac

Woods (see Parts List for exact dimensions)

- Fenders and roof: cherry, 1⁄2" thick (12mm):
- Chassis, engine, bed, backs, and side panels: oak, 3⁄4" thick (18mm)
- Bumpers: oak, 3⁄8" (9mm) thick
- Wooden dowels: 3⁄16" (5mm)-dia., 1⁄4" (6mm)-dia.
- Wooden axle pegs: 7⁄32" (5.6mm)-dia.

PARTS LIST: FLATBED TRUCK

	Part	Quantity	Materials	Dimensions
A	Chassis	1	Oak, 3⁄4" (18mm) thick	2 1⁄4" x 4 1⁄4" (5.7 x 10.8cm)
B	Axle pegs	4	7⁄32" (5.6mm)-dia., purchased	1 1⁄8" (2.9cm) long
C	Engine	2	Oak, 3⁄4" (18mm) thick	1" x 1 1⁄8" (2.5 x 2.9cm)
D	Bed	1	Oak, 3⁄4" (18mm) thick	2 1⁄2" x 3 1⁄2" (5.7 x 8.9cm)
E	Fenders	2	Cherry, 1⁄2" (12mm) thick	1 1⁄4" x 3 1⁄2" (3.2 x 8.9cm)
F	Bumpers	2	Oak, 3⁄8" (9mm) thick	3⁄4" x 3 1⁄2" (1.9 x 8.9cm)
G	Back	1	Oak, 3⁄4" (18mm) thick	3⁄4" x 3⁄4" x 3⁄4" (1.9 x 1.9 x 1.9cm)
H	Roof	1	Cherry, 1⁄2" (12mm) thick	2 1⁄4" x 1 3⁄4" (5.7 x 4.4cm)
I	Side panels	2	Oak, 3⁄4" (18mm) thick	2" x 2 1⁄2" (5.1 x 6.4cm)
J	Wheel, treaded	4	1 1⁄2" (3.8cm) dia., purchased	1⁄2" (12mm) thick
K	Bumper dowels	2	1⁄4" (6mm)-dia	3⁄4" (9mm) long
L	Roof dowels 1	2	1⁄4" (6mm)-dia.	1" (25mm) long
M	Roof dowels 2	2	3⁄16" (5mm)-dia.	1" (25mm) long

1 **Cut the blank for the chassis.**
Mark the holes for the axles and drill
1" (25mm) deep with a ⁷⁄₃₂" (5mm) drill bit.

2 Trace or adhere the patterns for
the sides on the blank. I cut a blank
about two and a half times the length of
a side so I can have a longer piece when
drilling the holes. Mark the location for the
¼" (6mm) holes in the sides. Set up the drill
press with a fence so the offset from the
edge is the same. Drill the ¼" (6mm) holes
in the sides 1½" (38mm) deep.

3 Use the same setup that was used
to drill the holes in the sides. Cut
a blank for the roof. Mark the locations for
the holes. Drill the ¼" (6mm) holes in the
front of the roof. Keep the drill press set up
and change to a ³⁄₁₆" (4mm) drill bit. Drill
the back holes in the roof.

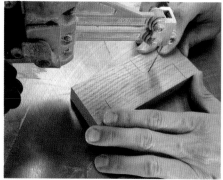

4 **Cut out the sides, engine, and spacer block.** Do this with a #7 skip-tooth blade
on the scroll saw. Glue these pieces together to make the cab of the truck. After the
glue has dried, use 100-grit sandpaper to round over and break the edges.

5 Make the bed of the truck by
cutting rabbets on each side. I used
my table saw to do this. First, I make a saw
cut on the bottom of the bed. This should
be the depth of the rabbet. Then, I rotate
the part 90 degrees so it is on the edge and
adjust the blade height. With the second
pass on the edge, cut out the scrap material.
Clean up the groove with a plane or 100-
grit sandpaper.

6 Cut a narrow strip of material for the bumpers. Mark and drill the holes for the bumper using a ¼" (6mm) drill bit. Glue the bumpers to the chassis. Drill ¼" (6mm) holes ¾" (19mm) deep using the holes in the bumper as a guide. Glue ¼" (6mm) dowels in the holes then sand the dowels flush to the bumpers.

7 Attach the roof to the cab by first inserting ¼" (6mm) dowels in the sides. These dowels should be cut oversized. Put the roof on the dowels and tap down so the roof is flush with the top of the sides. Use the ³⁄₁₆" (4mm) holes in the roof as guides to drill holes 1" (19 mm) deep. Glue ³⁄₁₆" (4mm) dowels in the holes.

8 Trace the profile of the roof on the side. Sand the profile to shape. Sand the bottom and back of the cab flat to remove any glue squeeze-out.

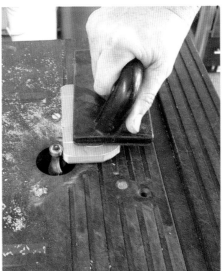

9 Glue the bed and cab to the chassis. The cab can sit flush to the bumper or set back ³⁄₁₆" (4mm). The bed will sit past the bumper. Clamp the parts together and let the glue dry.

10 Cut a blank for the fenders. Trace or adhere the patterns to the blank. Use a #5 skip-tooth blade to cut out the fenders. Use the wheels as guides to locate the position of the fenders. Glue the fenders in place.

11 Add finishing touches. Use 100-grit sandpaper to sand all faces of the toy and remove any sharp edges and corners. Finish sanding the toy with 220-grit sandpaper. Finish with child-safe finish or leave raw. Use axle pegs and attach the wheels once the finish is dry.

HELICOPTER

Patterns on pages 116–117

Whether reporting on news, following a car chase, or just zooming through the air for the joy of it, the helicopter provides kids with hours of high-flying fun. This toy is equipped with landing skids and propellers that spin, so you can take an afternoon of play to the next level. Small and compact, the design allows you to mix and match contrasting wood scraps for a classic, old-fashioned toy feel.

TOOLS & MATERIALS

- Scroll saw with blades: #3, #7 reverse-tooth
- Drill press with bits: ¼" (6mm), 7/32" (5.6mm)-dia.
- Sanders: spindle and belt
- Hammer
- Clamps
- Clear packaging tape
- Spray adhesive: repositionable
- White colored pencil (optional)
- Sandpaper: assorted grits up to 320

- Wood glue
- Child-safe finish, such as clear spray shellac

Woods (see Parts List for exact dimensions)

- Rotors, sides, tail, skids, skid platform: cherry, 5/16" (8mm) thick
- Body: oak, 1¼" (30mm) thick
- Wooden axle peg: 7/32" (5.6mm)-dia.

PARTS LIST: HELICOPTER

	Part	Quantity	Materials	Dimensions
A	Body	1	Oak, 1¼" (30mm) thick	2" x 4½" (5.1 x 11.4cm); compound-cut, per pattern
B	Rotor mount	1	Cherry, 5/16" (8mm) thick	1" (2.5cm) square
C	Top rotor	1	Cherry, 5/16" (8mm) thick	½" x 3¼" (1.3 x 8.3cm)
D	Tail rotor	1	Cherry, 5/16" (8mm) thick	½" x 1½" (1.3 x 3.8cm)
E	Tail	1	Cherry, 5/16" (8mm) thick	¾" x 1 5/16" (1.9 x 3.3cm)
F	Skids	2	Cherry, 5/16" (8mm) thick	5/16" x 2½" (0.8 x 6.4cm)
G	Skid platform	1	Cherry, 5/16" (8mm) thick	1" x 1¾" (2.5 x 4.4cm)
H	Sides	2	Cherry, 5/16" (8mm) thick	1½" x 2¼" (3.8 x 5.7cm)
I	Axle peg	1	7/32" (5.6mm)-dia. dowel	¾" (18mm) long

1 **Transfer the patterns and cut the body.** Drill a hole ¾" (1. 9cm) deep at the tail end, where indicated on the pattern. Use a ⁷⁄₃₂" (5. 6mm) -dia. bit. Cut the top view with a #7 reverse-tooth blade. Tape the curved waste back into place with clear packaging tape, then cut the side profile.

2 **Sand the body curves.** Use a spindle sander for the in-curving areas and a belt sander for the out-curving areas. Make sure the bottom of the helicopter body remains flat throughout the sanding process.

3 **Cut the remaining pieces.** Use a #3 reverse-tooth blade. Sand a slight bevel on the sides of the rotor mount, skid platform, and skids using the belt sander. Hand-sand all of the pieces, moving up progressively through the grits from 150 to 320. Ease all sharp edges and corners. Dry-fit the tail into the back slot. If the tail is too large, sand it down to size; if it is too thin, add a small piece of scrap as a wedge until the fit is tight.

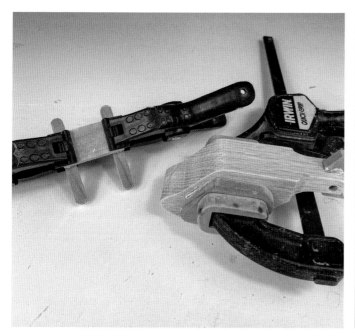

4 Glue and clamp the sides, body, and tail together. Then, do the same for the skid platform and skids.

5 Prepare the tail area. Using the same ⁷⁄₃₂" (5. 6mm)-dia. bit as before, deepen the existing hole in the side of the tail to ⅝" (1. 6cm).

6 Add the finishing touches. Glue and clamp the skid platform and propeller offset to the body. Attach the rotors with wooden axle pegs, coating just the bottom of each peg with wood glue and then securing them in place with a hammer. Then, finish the toy with two or three coats of a child-safe finish, such as clear spray shellac.

Stack 'Em Up

A few of the elements in this project can be cut en masse. It is more time efficient to cut multiples of the skids and sides than to scroll them individually.

BIPLANE

Patterns on pages 118–119

Biplanes stand as iconic symbols of aviation's early days, capturing the era of daring pilots and adventurous flights. These vintage aircraft have captured my interest as one of the first successful designs to fly. Whether admiring their graceful aerobatics or delving into the stories of pioneering aviators, the world of biplanes offers a captivating glimpse into the roots of aviation and the thrill of early airborne endeavors.

TOOLS & MATERIALS

- Table saw
- Scroll saw with #5, #7 skip-tooth blades
- Drill press with ¼", ⁷⁄₃₂", and ³⁄₁₆" (6mm, 5mm, 4mm) drill bits
- Router with ½" and ¼" (13mm and 6mm) roundover bits
- Sander with 100 and 150 grit sandpaper
- Miter saw
- Clamps
- Rubber bands
- Child-safe finish

Woods (see Parts List for exact dimensions)

- Wings, rudder, elevator, and propeller: wood of choice, ⁵⁄₁₆" (8mm) thick
- Fuselage: wood of choice, 1¼" (30mm) thick
- Wooden dowels: ³⁄₁₆" (5mm)-dia., ¼" (6mm)-dia.
- Axle peg: ¼" (6mm)-dia.

PARTS LIST: BIPLANE

	Part	Quantity	Materials	Dimensions
A	Wings	2	Wood of choice, ⁵⁄₁₆" (8mm) thick	1 ½" x 6" (3.8 x 15.2cm)
B	Rudder	1	Wood of choice, ⁵⁄₁₆" (8mm) thick	1 ¾" x 2" (4.4 x 5.1cm)
C	Elevator	1	Wood of choice, ⁵⁄₁₆" (8mm) thick	1 ¼" x 2 ½" (3.2 x 6.4cm)
D	Fuselage	1	Wood of choice, 1 ¼" (30mm) thick	(3.2 x 11.4cm)
E	Propeller	1	Wood of choice, ⁵⁄₁₆" (8mm) thick	½" x 2" (1.3 x 5.1cm)
F	Lower wing dowels	4	¼" (6mm)-dia.	2" (51mm) long
G	Fuselage dowels	3	³⁄₁₆" (5mm)-dia.	1" (25mm) long
H	Propeller axle peg	1	¼" (6mm)-dia.	1 ⅛" (2.9cm) long

1 **Prepare the materials.** Make the materials the appropriate thicknesses per the parts list. Only the rudder and propeller blanks need to be oversized. Mark the pattern on the fuselage. Mark the location for the wings. Cut the grooves for the wings in the fuselage. I use a table saw with a dado stack. Leave enough material the fuselage so you have enough room to safely handle the piece. The wings should fit snugly and flush with the plane body.

2 **Using a #7 skip-tooth blade, cut the rear angle most of the way through to the end.** Once the ½" (13mm) roundover is applied, it will be tough to know where to start the blade. Cut out the cockpit seat in the plane body.

3 **Use a ½" (13mm) roundover bit and a router to profile the bottom of the plane.** Use a ¼" (6mm) roundover to profile the top edges. After completing both profiles, finish cutting the angled piece from the tail section of the plane. Mark the location of the propeller at the end of the plane body. Drill a ⁷⁄₃₂" (5mm) hole in the end, about 1" (25mm) deep.

4 **Cut a ½" (13mm) strip about 5" (127mm) long.** Sand a 45-degree angle on one end. Cut this end off for the windshield. Glue the windshield on the fuselage.

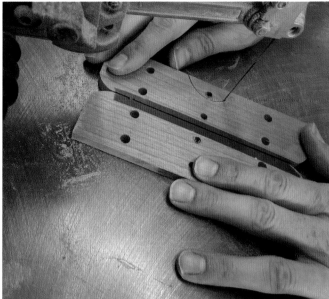

5 **Tape the wing blanks together so they can be drilled and cut out at the same time.** Mark the location for the ¼" (6mm) holes, and then drill. Mark the location for the ³⁄₁₆" (5mm) holes and only drill the front hole. Separate the wings and drill the second ³⁄₁₆" (5mm) hole in the lower wing. Mark and cut out the half circle in the upper wing.

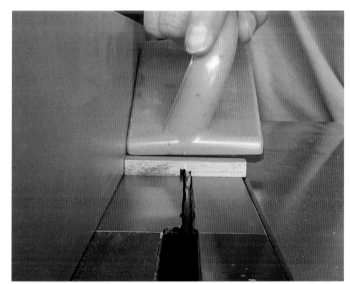

6 **Cut the groove in the lower tail section.** Do this using the table saw, raising the blade slightly. Using the fence, cut one side. Then, rotate the part 180 degrees and cut it again. I move the fence slightly and repeat until the vertical section fits snuggly in the groove. If you are not comfortable with this method, see an alternate way using dowels in the box on the next page. Trace and cut out the vertical wing. Cut out the profile on the lower tail wing.

7 **Trace the propeller and mark the hole.** Drill a ¼" (6mm) hole. Cut out using a #5 skip-tooth blade.

8 **Sand all the parts with 150-grit sandpaper to remove any tooling marks.** Cut four ¼" (6mm) dowels about 2" (51mm) long. Glue the dowels in the lower wing. Glue the lower wing in the groove on the fuselage. Make sure the wing is centered. Put glue in the ¼" (6mm) holes in the top wing. Put the top wing on the dowels. Tap the wing down until it is flush with the windshield.

Alternate Tail Wing Assembly

1 **Mark and drill ⅛" (3mm) holes in the lower wing section.** These should be ¼" (6mm) from the edge. Clamp the uncut vertical tail wing to a square block with bottom of the wing flush to the top.

2 **Clamp the lower tail wing section to the top of the block, centered on the tailpiece.** Use the holes to drill ¾" (19mm) deep holes in the vertical tailpiece. Then, unclamp the pieces. Finally, glue and insert ⅛" (3mm) dowels that are ⅝" (16mm) long into the lower tail wing. Sand the back side of the lower wing smooth. Cut out the parts to the tail wing. Glue the assembly together.

9 **Insert the dowels into the wings and fuselage.** Use the ³⁄₁₆" (5mm) holes in the wings as guides to drill ³⁄₁₆" (5mm) holes 1" (25mm) deep into the fuselage. Glue and insert 1" (25mm) long dowels. Cut or sand all dowels in the wings flush.

10 **Glue the tail section together.** Then, glue it to the fuselage. This is where the rubber bands come in handy, as it is difficult to clamp these parts down. Sand all the parts to 150 grit. Finish using a child-safe finish or leave the wood raw. Once finished, use an axle peg to put the propeller on.

GOLF CART

Patterns on pages 120–121

Bring a touch of the golf course to your child's playtime with this charming wooden golf cart. Designed to look just like the real thing, this toy golf cart is perfect for little golfers to transport their clubs and other golfing essentials around their imaginative course. Crafted from durable hardwoods, it combines realistic details with sturdy construction, ensuring it can withstand countless rounds of play. Whether it's for a young golf enthusiast or as a unique addition to a toy collection, this golf cart promises to drive plenty of fun and adventure.

TOOLS & MATERIALS

- Table saw
- Miter saw
- Scroll saw with #5 and #7 skip-tooth blades
- Drill press with ¼" and ⁷⁄₃₂" (6 and 5mm) drill bits
- Belt sander
- Hammer
- Spray adhesive: repositionable
- White colored pencil (optional)
- Clear packaging tape
- Sandpaper: assorted grits up to 320
- Wood glue
- Child-safe finish, such as clear spray shellac

Woods (see Parts List for exact dimensions)

- Fenders, chassis, seat back, roof, and front thin: cherry, ½" (12mm) thick
- Back and front thick: maple, ¾" (18mm) thick
- Seat bottom: cherry, ¼" (6mm) thick
- Wooden axle pegs: ⁷⁄₃₂" (5mm)-dia.
- Wooden treaded wheels: 1¼" (30mm)-dia.
- Wooden dowels: ³⁄₁₆" (5mm)-dia., ¼" (6mm)-dia.

PARTS LIST: GOLF CART

	Part	Quantity	Materials	Dimensions
A	Back	1	Maple, ¾" (18mm) thick	2 ½" x 2 ½" (6.4 x 6.4cm)
B	Front fenders	2	Cherry, ½" (12mm) thick	1 ¾" x 1" (4.4 x 2.5cm)
C	Back fenders	2	Cherry, ½" (12mm) thick	2 ⁷⁄₁₆" x 11/16" (6.2 x 1.7cm)
D	Chassis	1	Cherry, ½" (12mm) thick	5" x 3 ½" (12.7 x 8.9cm)
E	Seat bottom	1	Cherry, ¼" (6mm) thick	2 ½" x ¾" (6.4 x 1.9cm)
F	Seat back	1	Cherry, ½" (12mm) thick	2 ¼" x ⅞" (5.7 x 2.2cm)
G	Roof	1	Cherry, ½" (12mm) thick	4 ½" x 3 ½" (11.4 x 8.9cm)
H	Front thin	2	Cherry, ½" (12mm) thick	1 ⅜" x 1 ¼" (3.5 x 3.2cm)
I	Front thick	2	Maple, ¾" (18mm) thick	1 ⅜" x 1 ¼" (3.5 x 3.2cm)
J	Roof support dowels	4	¼" (6mm)-dia.	⅓" (0.8cm) long
K	Seat support dowels	4	³⁄₁₆" (5mm)-dia.	1 ½" (3.8cm) long
L	Wheels, treaded	4	1 ¼" (30mm)-dia., purchased	½" (1.3cm) thick
M	Axle pegs	4	⁷⁄₃₂" (5mm)-dia.	1 ⅛" (2.9cm)

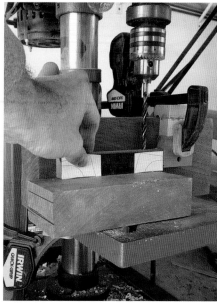

1 Transfer the patterns and cut the wood blanks to the given dimensions. Then, mark and drill ⁷⁄₃₂" (5mm) holes in the chassis. Drill the holes about 1¾" (45mm) deep. It is important that they be centered on the thickness of the part. This way, the same setup can be used to drill the front fenders. Mark the cutouts or adhere the chassis pattern to the chassis blank. Use a #5 skip-tooth blade to cut out the wheel well recesses.

2 Adhere the front and back fender plans to the blanks. Mark and drill the ¼" (6mm) holes in the front fenders. The holes should be about ⅜" (10mm) deep. Do not drill through the fender. Use a #5 skip-tooth blade to cut out the fenders.

3 Cut out the pieces for the front of the golf cart using a #7 skip-tooth blade. You will need two ¾" (19mm) thick pieces and two ½" (13mm) pieces. I made a quick template so I did not have to make a lot of copies. I also put tone woods in the middle to create a stripe in the middle. Glue the four pieces together. Use a sander to make sure all surfaces are even.

4 Rip a strip ¼" (6mm) thick from a ¾" (6mm)-thick board. This is for the seat bottom. Cut the strip to length and round the corners. Cut a blank for the seat back. Mark and drill ½" (13mm) deep holes in the seat back. Adhere the pattern to the seat back and cut it out using a #5 skip-tooth blade. Then, cut the back of the golf cart. Adhere the pattern to the blank. Drill the ³⁄₁₆" (4mm) holes all the way through, making sure they are in a straight line. Drill the ¼" (6mm) holes all the way through. Cut out the back using a #7 skip-tooth blade. Profile the back with a belt sander.

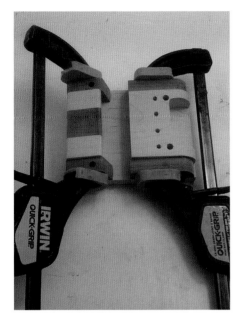

5 Sand all the pieces starting at 100 grit and finish with 150-grit sandpaper. Round the edges of the seat bottom and back. Glue the back and back fenders onto the chassis. Glue the front and the back fenders onto the chassis. Remove any glue squeeze-out and break all the edges with 150-grit sandpaper.

6 Install the seat and dowels. Cut four ³⁄₁₆" (4mm) dowels 1½" (38mm) long. Glue and insert the dowels in the back of the golf cart. Glue and tap the seat back onto the dowels until there is about ¼"–³⁄₈" (6–9mm) gap between the seat back and the top of the golf cart back. Glue the seat bottom in place and let it dry.

7 Cut the blank out for the roof. Mark and drill ¼" (6mm) holes. Sand to 150 grit. Cut four 5" (127mm) long pieces of ¼" (6mm) dowel. Gently tap in the front dowels into the fenders until they are seated. Tap the remaining two dowels in the back.

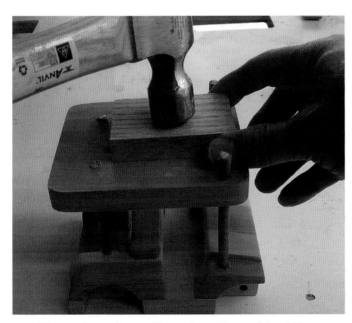

8 Glue and tap the roof into place. The roof should be parallel to the chassis. Cut and sand the dowels flush to the roof.

9 Sand all parts with 150-grit sandpaper. Break all sharp edges and corners. Finish with child-safe paint, clear coat, or leave the wood unfinished. After the finish has dried, attach the wheels using axle pegs.

SKID LOADER

Patterns on pages 122–124

Don't let its size fool you. This little skid loader is designed to handle dirt, grime, and rough play, just like on any construction site. It includes a strong arm made from two pieces of wood, and by using a table saw, you can make the entire thing from ¾" (18mm)-thick lumber. This cuts down on having to manage multiple thicknesses, so you can spend less time at the store and more time in the workshop.

TOOLS & MATERIALS

- Table saw
- Scroll saw with #5 skip-tooth blade
- Band saw (optional)
- Router with roundover bit: ¼" (6mm) radius
- Drill press with bits: 7/32" (5.5mm), ¼" (6mm), 3/8" (10mm)
- Belt sander
- Hammer (optional)
- Clamps
- Spray adhesive
- Blue painter's tape
- Sandpaper: 150-, 220-grit
- Wood glue

- Child-safe finish, such as clear spray shellac

Woods (see Parts List for exact dimensions)

- Cab front, cab sides, chassis, shovel arm, roof, and back: maple, ¾" (18mm) thick
- Lower arm, engine, shovel sides, and shovel bottom and top: walnut, ¾" (18mm) thick
- Wooden dowels: ¼" (6mm)-dia.
- Treaded wooden wheels: ½" (12mm) thick
- Wooden axle pegs: 7/32" (5.6mm)-dia.

PARTS LIST: SKID LOADER

	Part	Quantity	Materials	Dimensions
A	Chassis	1	Maple, ¾" (18mm) thick	3 ½" x 4" (8.9 x 10.2cm)
B	Cab sides	2	Maple, ¾" (18mm) thick	4" x 4 ½" (10.2 x 11.4cm)
C	Cab front	1	Maple, ¾" (18mm) thick	⅞" x 2" (2.2 x 5.1cm)
D	Cab roof	1	Maple, ¾" (18mm) thick	2" x 3" (5.1 x 7.6cm)
E	Cab back	1	Maple, ¾" (18mm) thick	2" x 3 ¾" (5.1 x 9.5cm)
F	Engine (glue-up of two)	1	Walnut, ¾" (18mm) thick	3 ¼" x 3 ½" (8.3 x 8.9cm)
G	Assembly dowels	14	¼" (6mm)-dia.	Cut to fit
H	Shovel top	1	Walnut, ¾" (18mm) thick	1" x 4 ¼" (2.5 x 10.8cm)
I	Shovel bottom	1	Walnut, ¾" (18mm) thick	2 ½" x 4 ¼" (6.4 x 10.8cm)
J K	Shovel sides	2	Walnut, ¾" (18mm) thick	1 ¾" x 3 ½" (4.4 x 8.9cm)
L M	Shovel arms	2	Maple, ¾" (18mm) thick	2 ¼" x 6 7/32" (5.7 x 15.8cm)
N	Lower arm	2	Walnut, ¾" (18mm) thick	½" x 2 11/32" (1.3 x 6cm)
O	Wheels, treaded	4	1 ½" (3.8cm)-dia., purchased	½" (12mm) thick
P	Axle pegs	8	7/32" (5.6cm)-dia.	1 ½" (3.8cm) long

1 **Transfer the patterns to the blanks.** Then, drill the holes for the cab sides. Use a ¼" (6mm)-dia. bit. Mark and drill ⁷⁄₃₂" (5. 5mm) holes in the chassis and engine. Then, cut the cab sides, engine, and chassis. *Note: I made the engine by gluing up two pieces of ¾" (1. 9cm) lumber and cutting the 45-degree angle on a band or table saw.*

2 **Profile the blanks for the cab front and roof.** Use a ¼" (6mm) roundover bit in a router. (You can also use a belt sander or pneumatic drum.) Then, cut the cab front, roof, and back.

3 **Assemble the cab.** Glue and clamp the cab pieces and chassis together. Once dry, drill ¼" (6mm) assembly dowel holes 1¼" (3. 2cm) deep in the areas indicated on the diagram. Cut a ¼" (6mm)-dia. dowel into 1⅜" (3. 5cm)-long pieces and insert them into the holes. (You may have to sand the dowels down.) Sand the surface smooth with 150-grit sandpaper. Then, glue the engine to the back of the cab and chassis.

4 **Drill the holes for the shovel parts.** Use a ¼" (6mm)-dia. bit for the fronts of the arms. Then, drill ⅜" (9mm) holes in the shovel sides and backs of the arms, going only halfway through the blank. Drill ¼" (6mm) holes in the center of the ⅜" holes through the shovel sides, going all the way through the blank.

5 **Cut the arm grooves.** Use a table saw. Then, cut out the scoop arms and shovel sides. Drill ⁷⁄₃₂" (5. 5mm) holes in the lower arm blank and then cut the lower arms.

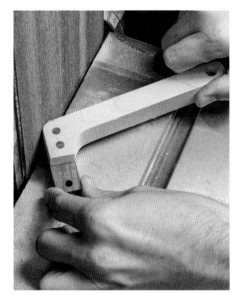

6 **Glue the lower arms into the upper arm grooves.** The holes on the lower arms face outside. Cut four 1⅛" (2.9cm) pieces from the ¼" (6mm) dowel and insert them into the dowel holes. Sand the surface of each arm flush; I used 150-grit sandpaper in a belt sander.

7 **Cut the shovel groove details.** Use a table saw. Cut the shovel bottom groove detail on one side and the shovel top groove detail on the other. Then, cut the pieces to size. *Note: Use a push stick as needed for safety.*

8 **Dry-fit the arms to the body.** Then, fit the shovel bottom and back assembly between the arms. Trim the assembly if needed.

9 **Glue and clamp the shovel sides onto the assembly.** When dry, sand all sides flush with 220-grit sandpaper, creating bevels in the shovel bottom and back. Round the edges slightly. Use the belt sander.

10 **Finish all the parts.** Use a child-safe finish, such as shellac. Once dry, attach the arms to the engine, gluing ⁷⁄₃₂" (5.5mm)-dia. axle pegs in the holes. Attach the shovel, gluing a ⁷⁄₃₂" (5.5mm)-dia. axle peg in the lower arm hole on each side. You may need to cut the length down so the heads fit into the holes. Use a hammer to secure them, if necessary.

TOW TRUCK

Patterns on pages 125–128

This sturdy tow truck is a blast to build and even more fun to play with. The durable design includes a movable crane arm, functional wheels, and a reinforced wooden hook—making it perfect for rescuing and transporting vehicles in need.

	Part	Quantity	Materials	Dimensions
	PARTS LIST: TOW TRUCK			
A	Cab sides	2	Maple, ¾" (18mm) thick	4 ¼" x 5 ¼" (10.8 x 13.3cm)
B	Cab hood	3 (glued together)	Maple, ¾" (18mm) thick	2" x 2 ½" (5.1 x 6.4cm) Note: The starting length for this piece is approx. 5" (12.7cm); finished length is 2 ½" (6.4cm).
C	Cab roof	1	Maple, ¾" (18mm) thick	2" x 2 ¼" (5.1 x 5.7cm)
D	Cab back	1	Maple, ¾" (18mm) thick	2" x 2 ¾" (5.1 x 7cm)
E	Chassis	1	Maple, ¾" (18mm) thick	2 ½" x 10 ⅜" (6.4 x 26.4cm)
F	Crane arm	1	Maple, ¾" (18mm) thick	3 ⅛" x 5" (7.9 x 12.7cm)
G	Bed sides	2	Walnut, ¾" (18mm) thick	2 ¾" x 4 ⅞" (7 x 12.4cm)
H	Bed	1	Walnut, ¾" (18mm) thick	4 ⅝" x 4 ⅞" (11.8 x 12.4cm)
I	Bed back	1	Walnut, ¾" (18mm) thick	2 ¼" x 3 3⁄16" (5.7 x 8.1cm)
J	Hook	1	Walnut, ¾" (18mm) thick	1 ½" x 3" (3.8 x 7.6cm)
K	Cab steps	2	Walnut, ¾" (18mm) thick	7⁄16" x 2 ⅞" (1.1 x 7.3cm)
L	Fenders	2	Walnut, ¾" (18mm) thick	1 ½" x 2 ⅞" (3.8 x 7.3cm)
M	Assembly/headlight dowels	1	¼"-dia. (6mm)	24" (61cm) long (cut to fit)
N	Wheel axle pegs	4	7⁄32"-dia. (5.6mm)	1 ⅛" (2.9cm) long
O	Arm axle pegs	2	11⁄32"-dia. (8.7mm)	1 13⁄16" (4.6cm) long
P	Wheels, treaded	6	1 ½" (3.8cm)-dia., purchased	½" thick (12mm)

TOOLS & MATERIALS

- Table saw
- Scroll saw with #7 skip-tooth blade
- Router with roundover bits: ¼" (6mm), ⅜" (10mm)-dia.
- Drill press with bits: ½" (12.7mm), ⁷⁄₃₂" (5.6mm), ¼" (6mm), ¹¹⁄₃₂" (8.7mm), ⅜" (10mm), ⁵⁄₁₆" (8mm)
- Sanders: belt, pneumatic drum (optional)
- Hammer
- Clamps
- Vise
- Vacuum
- Spray adhesive
- Blue painter's tape, clear packaging tape
- Sandpaper: assorted grits to 220
- Wood glue

- Child-safe finish, such as shellac or beeswax and walnut oil

Woods (see Parts List for exact dimensions)

- Cab hood, cab sides, roof, chassis, crane arm, and back: maple, ¾" (18mm) thick
- Bed, bed sides, bed back, hook, cab steps, and fenders: walnut, ¾" (18mm) thick
- Wooden dowels: ¼" (6mm)-dia., ½" (12mm)-dia.
- Wooden axle pegs: ⁷⁄₃₂" (5.6mm)-dia., ¹¹⁄₃₂" (8.7mm)-dia.
- Treaded wooden wheels: 1½" (3.8cm)-dia.

All dimensions are exact; if desired, add extra clearance to each blank for ease of cutting

1 **Transfer the patterns to the blanks.** Then, drill the holes. Secure the first cab side blank in a vise with the front facing up, and use a ½" (1.3cm)-dia. bit to drill the hole for the headlights. Repeat on the second side. Use a ¼" (6mm)-dia. bit for the dowel holes on the side of the cab and the roof, and to drill a blade-entry hole in the corner of the truck window. Use a 7/32" (5.6mm)-dia. bit to drill the hole for the front wheel axle in the same blank. Then, using a scroll saw and a #7 blade, cut out the truck window. Next, cut the cab side and chassis perimeters. Drill the hole for the rear wheel axle on the chassis with the 7/32" (5.6mm)-dia. bit.

2 **Make the cab hood.** Glue up three pieces of ¾" (1.9cm)-thick stock to make a block that is at least 5" (12.7cm) long. *Note: I find it best to make the cab hood a bit longer than needed so as to have more to grip when sawing.* Clamp and let dry. Then, cut the width to size. It should sit snugly between the side panels when dry-fit on the chassis.

3 **Cut the grill grooves.** I used a table saw, but you could use the scroll saw, if preferred. On one end of the cab hood, mark five evenly spaced grooves for the grill. Cut the grooves. Then, cut the block so it measures 2½" (6.4cm) long. Sand the surface smooth; I used a belt sander with a 150-grit belt.

4 **Profile the front edge of the roof.** Use a ¼" (6mm)-dia. roundover bit in a router. You could also use a pneumatic drum. Leave the roof and back attached until the front edge is profiled. Then, cut both pieces to length.

5 Make the fenders. Use the scroll saw to cut out the fenders. Profile the edges with a ⅜" (10mm)-dia. roundover bit in the router. Then, cut the cab steps on the scroll saw at a 15-degree angle.

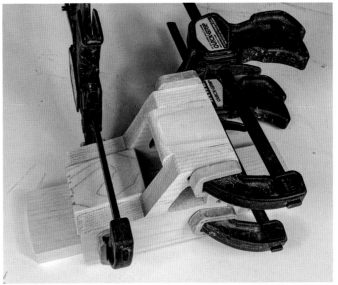

6 Assemble the truck cab. Use the chassis as a reference while gluing the cab sides, hood, back, and roof together. *Note: Do not glue the chassis to the cab at this time.* Clamp and let dry.

7 Add the assembly dowels. Cut eight 1¼" (3. 2cm) long pieces from the ¼" (6mm)-dia. dowel. Insert them into the dowel holes and secure them into place with a hammer. Sand the surface smooth with 150-grit sandpaper. Then, glue the chassis to the truck cab. Clamp and let dry overnight.

8 Add the wheels. Insert a ⁷⁄₃₂" (5. 6mm)-dia. axle peg into the wheel. Then, insert the peg into the axle hole, using the hammer to secure it. Glue on the fenders and truck steps. Then cut two ½" (1. 3cm)-long pieces from the ¼" (6mm)-dia. dowel for the headlights. Add glue to the ends, and then lightly tap them into place with the hammer (you'll tighten them later). Sand the assembly with 150-grit sandpaper.

9 **Make the hook.** Drill a 5/16" (8mm)-dia. hole in the top of the hook. Then, drill a ¼" (6mm)-dia. hole in the edge. Glue a ¼" (6mm)-dia. dowel into the hole to provide added towing strength. Then, cut the front pattern view. Once done, hold the workpiece and the waste in place and vacuum away the dust. Wrap the entire block (waste and all) in clear packaging tape, rotate the blank, and cut the side pattern view. Sand the surface smooth with 150-grit sandpaper.

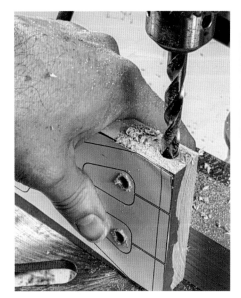

10 **Cut the crane arm.** Use the ¼" (6mm)-dia. bit to drill the holes on the sides and the blade-entry holes in the front. Cut the shape on the scroll saw. *Note: You will cut the slots at the bottom later.* Sand the surface smooth with 150-grit sandpaper. Attach the hook with a ¼" (6mm)-dia. dowel. The hook should swing freely. Remove material if needed.

11 **Cut grooves for the bottom sides of the truck bed.** Use the table saw.

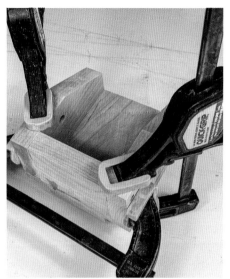

12 **Make the sides of the truck bed.** Drill two assembly dowel holes with the ¼" (6mm)-dia. bit. Then drill the center ⅜" (9mm)-dia. countersink hole through. Drill the outer ½" (1.3cm)-dia. countersink hole about ⅜" (9mm) deep, as indicated on the pattern. Cut the shape on the scroll saw. Then, sand the surface smooth with 150-grit sandpaper. Repeat on the other side.

13 **Dry-fit the truck bed assembly.** Then, glue the sides, back, and bed together. Clamp and let dry. Glue in the assembly dowels and secure them with the hammer. Sand the surface smooth with 150-grit sandpaper. Glue the bed to the rest of the truck.

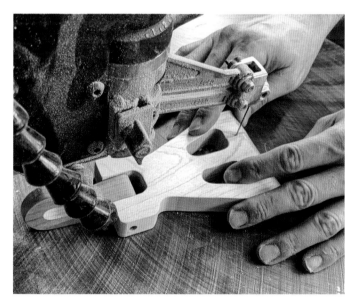

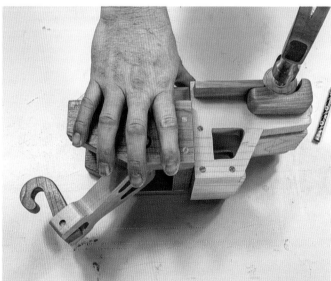

14 **Cut the slots in the crane.** Use the scroll saw. *Note: It is important to do this after attaching the hook because the slots may cause the arm to break when inserting the dowel to hold the hook.* Pinch the sides together and slide the arm into the truck bed. Secure the arm with the ¹¹⁄₃₂" (8.7mm)-dia. axle pegs.

15 **Apply a finish.** Use a child-safe finish, such as shellac. Use the hammer to fully secure the pegs.

TRACTOR

Patterns on pages 129–131

I enjoy making toys that generations of children can play with. This tractor features a small, sturdy frame with wheels that allow it to move around on various surfaces. It also comes with a detachable trailer and a harrow. Playing with a toy tractor can be a fun way for children to explore their imaginations and learn about farming. It can also help develop their motor skills and hand-eye coordination as they move the toy around.

	Part	Quantity	Materials	Dimensions
	PARTS LIST: TRACTOR			
A	Tractor sides	1	Cherry, ½" (12mm) thick	3 ¼" x 4 ½" (8.3 x 11.4cm)
B	Roof	1	Cherry, ½" (12mm) thick	2" x 3 ½" (5.1 x 8.9cm)
C	Front axle	1	Cherry, ½" (12mm) thick	1" x 3" (2.5 x 7.6cm)
D	Harrow sides	1	Cherry, ½" (12mm) thick	1 ¼" x 2" (3.2 x 5.1cm)
E	Wagon sides	1	Cherry, ½" (12mm) thick	1 ¼ x 4" (3.2 x 10.2cm)
F	Wagon front	1	Cherry, ½" (12mm) thick	1 ¼" x 3 29/32" (3.2 x 9.9cm)
G	Wagon bottom	1	Cherry, ½" (12mm) thick	4" (10.2cm) square
H	Chassis	1	Oak, ¾" (18mm) thick	2" x 6 ½" (5.1 x 16.5cm)
I	Harrow hitch	1	Oak, ¾" (18mm) thick	1" x 3 ¾" (2.5 x 9.5cm)
J	Fenders	2	Oak, ¾" (18mm) thick	2 ⅛" x 3 ⅛" (5.4 x 7.9cm)
K	Engine	2	Oak, ¾" (18mm) thick	1 ½" x 2 ½" (3.8 x 6.4cm)
L	Seat base	1	Oak, ¾" (18mm) thick	1 ¾" x 2" (4.4 x 5.1cm)
M	Seat bottom	1	Oak, ¾" (18mm) thick	¾" x 1" (1.9 x 2.5cm)
N	Seat back	1	Oak, ¾" (18mm) thick	1" x 1 ¾" (2.5 x 4.4cm)
O	Wagon hitch	1	Oak, ¾" (18mm) thick	2" x 1 ¼" (5.1 x 3.2cm)
P	Assembly dowels	1	Poplar, ¼"-dia. (6mm)	8" (30.5cm) long (cut to fit)
Q	Assembly dowels	1	Poplar, ⁵⁄₁₆"-dia. (8mm)	1 ¾" (4.4cm) long (cut to fit)
R	Assembly dowels	2	Poplar, ⅜"-dia. (9mm)	4 ¾" (12.1cm) long (cut to fit)
S	Assembly dowels	1	Poplar, ½"-dia. (12mm)	1 ½" (3.8cm) long (cut to fit)
T	Wooden wheels	10	1 ½"-dia. (3.8cm)	⁷⁄₁₆" (1.1cm) thick
U	Wooden wheels	2	2 ¾"-dia. (7cm)	⁹⁄₁₆" (14mm) thick
V	Axle pegs	4	⁷⁄₃₂"-dia. (5.6mm)	1 ⅛" (2.9cm)long
W	Axle pegs	2	¹¹⁄₃₂"-dia. (9mm)	1 ¹³⁄₁₆" (4.6cm) long
X	Wagon Axle	1	Cherry ½" (12mm) thick	¾" x 4" (1.9 x 10.2cm)

TOOLS & MATERIALS

- Table saw
- Scroll saw with #7 skip-tooth blade
- Palm sander
- Belt sander (optional)
- Pneumatic drum sander (optional)
- Clamps
- Drill press
- Drill with bits: 7/32" (5.6mm), 1/4" (6mm), 5/16" (8mm), 11/32" (9mm), 3/8" (10mm), and 1/2" (13mm)-dia.
- Router with assorted bits
- Hand plane
- Tape: clear packaging, painter's
- Spray adhesive
- Tracing paper (optional)
- Pencil
- Wood glue
- Cyanoacrylate (CA) glue

- Sandpaper: assorted grits
- Child-safe acrylic paints (optional)
- Finish, such as shellac

Woods (see Parts List for exact dimensions)

- Tractor sides, roof, front axle, harrow sides, wagon sides, wagon front, wagon bottom: cherry, 1/2" thick (12mm)
- Chassis, harrow hitch, fender, engine, seat base, seat bottom, wagon hitch, and seat back: oak, 3/4" thick (18mm)
- Wooden dowels: 1/4" (6mm)-dia., 5/16" (8mm)-dia., 3/8" (9mm)-dia., 1/2" (12mm)-dia.
- Treaded wooden wheels: 1 1/2" (3.8cm)-dia., 2 3/4" (7cm_-dia.
- Wooden axle pegs: 7/32" (5.6mm)-dia., 11/32" (9mm)-dia.

Making the Tractor

1 **Transfer the patterns and begin cutting.** Prepare the sides, chassis, and fenders. Note the location of the holes on the patterns. Drill a ⁵⁄₁₆" (8mm)-dia. hole in the chassis. Drill the holes in the front axle, which are ¼" (6mm)-dia. on the face and ⁷⁄₃₂" (5.6cm)-dia. on the ends. Then, drill the ¹¹⁄₃₂" (9mm)-dia. holes in the sides and the ¼" (6mm)-dia. holes in the seat bottom.

2 **Form the engine.** Cut the two pieces on the scroll saw, angling the table or arm as indicated in the patterns. Wipe off excess dust with a cloth, and glue and clamp the pieces. Let dry. Sand the faces smooth, and use a router or a pneumatic drum sander to round over the top edges.

3 **Make the seat.** Glue the seat bottom and seat back together, and clamp until dry. When dry, glue the seat to the seat base on the chassis. Use the holes in the seat base as a guide and drill the holes to 1¼" (3.2cm) deep. Cut ¼" (6mm) dowels and insert them into the holes. Sand the dowels flush with the base.

4 **Assemble the tractor body.** Sand all parts to 150-grit. Smooth all inside edges. Use a ¼" (6mm) roundover bit or a belt sander to soften the edges of the roof. Glue the seat base assembly and sides to the chassis. The back of the sides and seat base should line up with the back points on the chassis. Glue the roof to the sides. Clamp all the parts together so they don't shift while drying, and let dry completely before proceeding.

5 **Attach the axle.** When the tractor body is dry, use the sides as a guide and drill ¹¹⁄₃₂" (9mm)-dia. holes into the chassis, 1¼" (3. 2cm) deep. Glue the front axle onto the chassis. Set the axle back ¼" (6mm) from the front edge of the chassis and center it. Using the holes in the axle as a guide, drill holes 1¼" (3. 2cm) deep. Insert the dowels and sand them flush.

6 **Attach the fenders.** Use the wheels as a guide for placement. The fenders should extend past the back of the sides and sit flush with the bottom of the sides. There will be about a ⅛" (3mm) gap between the fender and the wheel. Glue and clamp the fenders onto the sides.

7 **Make the exhaust stack.** Cut a ½" (1. 3cm) dowel 1½" (3. 8cm) long and a ⁵⁄₁₆" (8mm) dowel 1¼" (3. 2cm) long. Use a hand plane or sander to create a flat end on the ½" (1. 3cm) dowel. Drill a ⁵⁄₁₆" (8mm) hole ⅜" (9mm) deep at the end of the ½" (1. 3cm) dowel. Glue the ⁵⁄₁₆" (8mm) dowel into the ½" (1. 3cm)-dia. dowel. Then, glue this assembly to the right side of the tractor. *Note: You can drill a ½" (1. 3cm) hole partway through a piece of scrap and drill a pilot hole in the center.* This can be used to mark the center of the ½" (1. 3cm) dowel to drill.

Making the Harrow

1 **Prepare the harrow.** Referring to the pattern, drill the ⅜" (9mm) and ¼" (6mm) harrow hitch holes in the top and ⅜" (9mm) and ⁵⁄₁₆" (8mm)-dia. holes in the harrow sides. Cut two pieces of ⅜" (9mm) dowel 4 ¾" (12. 1cm) long and one piece of ¼" (6mm) dowel 5 ⅞" (15cm) long.

2 **Assemble the harrow.** Glue two ⅜" (9mm) dowels into one side of the harrow. Slide the harrow hitch so it is in the middle of the dowels and use cyanoacrylate (CA) glue to affix it into place. Glue the other side to the ends of the dowels. Let this assembly dry thoroughly, and then sand to smooth and soften all edges.

Making the Wagon

1 **Prepare the wagon.** Use a table saw to cut a 20-degree angle on both sides of the wagon. Then, cut a 20-degree angle on each end of the wagon front. Alternatively, you could make the angled cut with a scroll saw, tilting the arm or table to 20 degrees. Drill ⁷⁄₃₂" (5. 6mm)-dia. holes at each end of the wagon's axle. Drill a ¼" (6mm)-dia. hole in the hitch blank.

2 **Glue up the wagon.** Glue the sides, front, and bottom together. Start by gluing the front to the bottom and clamp them together. Then glue the sides on. Clamp the sides to the front using some scraps cut at a 20-degree angle. Then, clamp the sides to the bottom. When this assembly is completely dry, center the axle on the bottom and glue it to that piece. Center the hitch on the front of the wagon flush to the top and glue both pieces in place.

Assembling and Finishing

1 **Sand all pieces to 150-grit.** You can leave this project completely natural or finish in several ways. If you do choose to finish the project, do so before assembling. I like the natural look of wood, so I typically apply a clear coat of shellac, since it is child-safe. If you prefer a colorful tractor, use child-safe acrylic paints. When all the pieces are completely dry, assemble the tractor, harrow, and wagon. Attach the 2¾" (7cm)-dia. wheels to the rear of the tractor and 1½" (3. 8cm)-dia. wheels to the front of the tractor using axle pegs and glue.

2 **Complete the harrow.** To make the harrow, attach one 1½" (3. 8cm)-dia. wheel to the end of the ¼" (6mm) dowel from Step 2, Making the Harrow. Run this through the hole on the harrow, and then put four 1½" (3. 8cm) wheels on the dowel before running it through the other end. Glue a 1½" (3. 8cm) wheel onto the other side of the harrow. Space the wheels evenly on the dowel and glue them into place. I used cyanoacrylate (CA) glue for the middle four wheels. Lightly sand the middle of the ¼" (6mm) dowel so the wheels move freely.

3 **Attach the 1½" (3. 8cm)-dia. wheels to the wagon with axle pegs and glue.** Finish by attaching the wheels to the wagon with axle pegs. Insert ¼" (6mm) dowels in the harrow and wagon hitch.

GARBAGE TRUCK

Patterns on pages 132–135

This wooden garbage truck isn't just a toy—it's a great way to encourage kids to clean up after an afternoon of play. And while it's on the larger side, this mobile marvel can run circles around its store-bought counterparts because it's built to be used, and to last. Use whichever hardwood varieties are accessible to you; I chose the understated tones of maple and oak.

	Part	Quantity	Materials	Dimensions
	PARTS LIST: GARBAGE TRUCK			
A	Cab front	1	Oak, ¾" (18mm) thick	2 ¾" x 3" (7 x 7.6cm)
B	Cab back	1	Oak, ¾" (18mm) thick	2" x 6" (5.1 x 15.2cm)
C	Cab sides	2	Oak, ¾" (18mm) thick	4 ½" x 5 ½" (11.4 x 14cm)
D	Bumper	1	Oak, ¼" (6mm) thick	⅞" x 5 ½" (2.2 x 14cm)
E	Cab bottom	1	Oak, ¾" (18mm) thick	3" (7.6cm) square
F	Cab top	1	Oak, ¾" (18mm) thick	2" x 3" (5.1 x 7.6cm)
G	Wheel spacers	2	Maple, ¾" (18mm) thick	1 ⅛" x 5 ¼" (2.9 x 13.3cm)
H	Chassis beams	2	Maple, ¾" (18mm) thick	1 ⅛" x 15" (2.9 x 38.1cm)
I	Chassis spacers	6	Maple, ¾" (18mm) thick	1 ⅛" x 1 ½" (2.9 x 3.8cm)
J	Wheel well	1	Maple, ¾" (18mm) thick	6" x 7" (15.2 x 17.8cm)
K	Compactor front	1	Oak, ¾" (18mm) thick	1 ⅛" x 15" (2.9 x 38.1cm)
L	Compactor sides	2	Oak, ¾" (18mm) thick	4" x 6 ¾" (10.2 x 17.1cm)
M	Compactor bottom	1	Oak, ¾" (18mm) thick	4 ½" x 7" (11.4 x 17.8cm)
N	Compactor top	1	Oak, ¾" (18mm) thick	3" x 5 ½" (7.6 x 14cm)
O	Container bottom	1	Oak, ¾" (18mm) thick	4 ½" x 7" (11.4 x 17.8cm)
P	Container top	1	Oak, ¾" (18mm) thick	4 ½" x 7 ¹³⁄₁₆" (11.4 x 19.8cm)
Q	Container sides	2	Oak, ¾" (18mm) thick	5 ½" x 7" (14 x 17.8cm)
R	Back hinge	1	Oak, ¾" (18mm) thick	5 ½" x 6" (14 x 15.2cm)
S	Container back	1	Oak, ¾" (18mm) thick	5 ½" x 6" (14 x 15.2cm)
T	Lift arms	2	Oak, ¾" (18mm) thick	5 ⅝" x 6 ¼" (14.3 x 15.9cm)
U	Arm stretcher	1	Oak, ¾" (18mm) thick	2 ½" x 5 ⅝" (6.4 x 14.3cm)
V	Dumpster sides	2	Oak, ¾" (18mm) thick	4" (10.2cm) square
W	Dumpster bottom	1	Oak, ¾" (18mm) thick	2 ½" x 4 ⅛" (6.4 x 10.5cm)
X	Dumpster back	1	Oak, ¾" (18mm) thick	4" x 4 ⅛" (10.1 x 10.5cm)
Y	Dumpster front	1	Oak, ¾" (18mm) thick	3 ⁵⁄₃₂" x 4 ⅛" (8 x 10.5cm)
Z	Dumpster arm slots	2	Oak, ¾" (18mm) thick	1" x 4" (2.5 x 10.2cm)
AA	Assembly dowels	50	¼" (6mm)-dia.	1 ¼" (30mm) long
AB	Fork dowels	2	⅜" (9mm)-dia.	2 ¾" (7cm) long
	Axle pegs (cab & lift arms)	4	¹¹⁄₃₂" (9mm)-dia.	1 ¹³⁄₁₆" (4.6cm) long
	Axle pegs (dual wheels)	4	¹¹⁄₃₂" (9mm)-dia.	2 ⅛" (5.4cm) long
AC	Axle pegs (dumpster)	4	⁷⁄₃₂" (5.5mm)-dia.	1 ¼" (30mm) long
	Wheels, treaded	2	2" (5.1cm)-dia.	¾" (1.9cm) thick
	Dual treaded wheels	4	2" (5.1cm)-dia.	1 ½" (3.8cm)thick
AD	Wheels, treaded (dumpster)	4	⅞" (2cm)-dia.	⅜" (9.5mm) thick

- Table saw
- Scroll saw with blades: #7 skip-tooth
- Drill press with bits: ¼" (6mm), ⁷⁄₃₂" (5.5mm), ⁹⁄₃₂" (7mm), ¹¹⁄₃₂" (9mm), ⅜" (10mm)-dia.
- Router with bits: ⅜" (10mm) roundover, 45° chamfer
- Belt sander
- Pneumatic drum sander (optional)
- Hammer
- Clamps
- Vise
- Chisel of choice
- Spray adhesive
- Blue painter's tape
- Sandpaper: assorted grits up to 320
- Wood glue
- Finish: clear shellac (or other child-safe finish)

Woods (see Parts List for exact dimensions)

- Cab parts, compactor parts, container parts, dumpster parts, back hinge, lift arms, arm stretcher: oak, ¾" (18mm) thick
- Bumper: oak, ¼" (6mm) thick
- Wheel spacers, chassis beams, chassis spacers, and wheel well: maple, ¾" (18mm) thick
- Wooden dowels: ¼" (6mm)-dia., ⅜" (10mm)-dia.
- Wooden axle pegs: ⁷⁄₃₂" (5.6mm)-dia., ¹¹⁄₃₂" (9mm)-dia.
- Treaded wooden wheels: ¾" (18mm)-dia, ⅞" (2cm)-dia.

All dimensions are exact; if desired, add extra clearance to each blank for ease of cutting

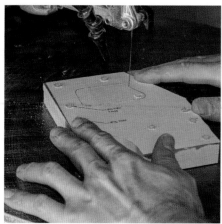

1 **Transfer the patterns to the blanks.** Cut the cab sides to size using a table saw. Then, drill the ¼" (6mm) and ¹¹⁄₃₂" (9mm)-dia. holes in the sides as noted in the pattern. *Note: I have found it easier to avoid drilling all the way through, as this avoids blowout.* Make the remaining cuts using a scroll saw with a #7 skip-tooth blade.

2 **Cut the cab top, front, back, and bottom.** Profile one end of the front and top pieces on a router with a ⅜" (10mm) roundover bit. Alternatively, you could round those edges on a pneumatic drum sander.

3 **Cut the bumper.** Assemble the cab so that the bottom sits 1½" (3. 8cm) up from the bottom of the side. Glue the pieces together with wood glue, clamp, and let dry. Then, drill two evenly spaced ¼" (6mm)-dia. dowel holes through the bumper, 1⅛" (2. 9cm) deep. Deepen the dowel holes in the cab sides until they are roughly 1⅛" (2. 9cm) deep. Cut a ¼" (6mm) wood dowel into pieces slightly longer than the hole depth and glue them into the dowel holes. Sand smooth with a belt sander.

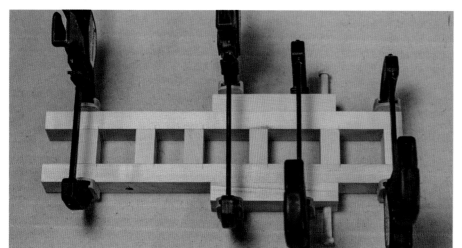

4 **Cut the chassis beam, chassis spacers, and wheel spacers.** Use the table saw. Mark the locations of the spacers, glue and clamp the chassis beam and chassis spacers together, and let dry. Drill the ¹¹⁄₃₂" (9mm)-dia. holes into the wheel spacers and line the holes up with those on the beam. *Note: I use axle pegs to ensure the holes are aligned.* Then, glue and clamp on the wheel spacers. Hand-sand the pieces, moving up progressively through the grits from 150 to 320. Glue the cab to the chassis so the inside of the cab front meets the front of the chassis assembly.

5 **Cut the container bottom, top, sides, back, and back hinge.** Then, cut the compactor front, sides, bottom, and top. Mark and drill the ¼" (6mm)-dia. holes on the container sides and back, as well as the compactor sides. Mark the angles on the compactor sides and cut them on the table saw.

6 Cut the wheel well and then add the grooves. Hand-sand smooth.

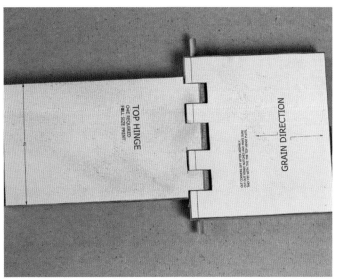

7 Drill the holes for the hinge. The holes in the sides of the top hinge (⁹⁄₃₂" [7mm]-dia.) will need to be slightly larger than those in the sides of the back hinge (¼" [6mm]-dia.) to allow the back door to swing open and shut. Round over the back hinge and container top with a ⅜" (10mm) roundover bit or a pneumatic drum sander. Dry-fit the hinge elements to ensure they can move without rubbing.

8 Profile the top edge of the compactor sides and container bottom. I used a 45-degree chamfer bit in the router, but you can use a pneumatic drum sander if desired.

9 Assemble the compactor and container. Glue and clamp the pieces together and let dry. Drill the ¼" (6mm)-dia. dowel holes 1⅛" (2. 9cm) deep. Then, cut ¼" (6mm)-dia. dowels slightly longer than the hole depth and glue in place. Do not place dowels in the hinged part yet. Sand the parts smooth on the belt sander.

10 Clamp the assembled back and container together. Chamfer the four edges of the container from front to back. Use the table saw. Then, unclamp the pieces and add a 45-degree chamfer to the face of the back piece. Glue the wheel well to the bottom of the container.

11 **Cut the lift arms to size.** Use the scroll saw. Then, drill a ⅜" (10mm) hole with a ½" (13mm) counterbore ⅜" (10mm) deep on the side of the arm as noted on the pattern, making sure you have a left and right side arm. Drill the ⅜" (10mm) hole in the face of the arm (for the forks) and the remaining holes. Sand the pieces smooth to 220 grit.

12 **Cut the arm stretcher.** It will be ⅛" (3mm) wider than the cab assembly to allow the arms to move up and down without rubbing against the sides. Glue and clamp it flush with the bottom of the lift arms. Then, drill ¼" (6mm)-dia. holes through the sides of the lift arms and into the stretcher, 1⅛" (2. 9cm) deep. Cut ¼" (6mm)-dia. dowels into 1¼" (3. 2cm)-long pieces, apply glue, and insert them into the holes. Let dry and sand the assembly on the belt sander until the dowels are flush with the sides.

13 **Cut the dumpster sides, bottom, back, front, and slot.** Drill the 1" (2. 5cm) wheel depressions ½" (1. 3cm) deep. Trim out the bottom corners of the wheel depressions with a chisel. Drill the remaining 1⅛" (2. 9cm)-deep holes for the dowels and axle pegs, referring to the patterns. *Note: The ¼" (6mm)-dia. holes are for dowels and the ⁷⁄₃₂" (5. 5mm)-dia. holes are for axle pegs.* Cut the bevel on the table saw.

14 **Glue and clamp the dumpster pieces together.** Cut and glue in pieces of ¼" (6mm)-dia. dowel. Let dry and smooth on the belt sander until the back of the dumpster is flush with the sides and the dowels sit flush with each surface.

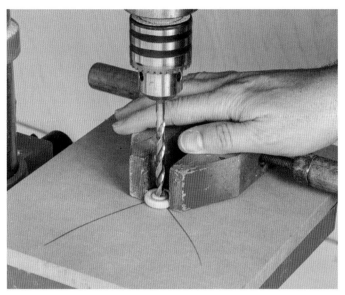

15 **Prepare the wheels.** Clamp each ⅞" (2. 2cm)-dia. wheel in a vise and redrill the center holes to ¼" (6mm). Drill the dumpster slot holes.

16 **Add the finishing touches.** Glue the ⅜" (10mm)-dia. fork dowels into the front of the lift arms. Dry-fit the wheels and axle pegs on the chassis, the lift arms onto the cab, and the wheels onto the dumpster. Place the dumpster slots on the forks and glue them into position on the dumpster. *Note: Don't glue the forks to the slots, as the dumpster is removable.*

17 **Sand all parts to 150 grit and soften any sharp edges.** Tape off the bottom of the wheel well, the bottom of the compactor, and the top of the chassis with painter's tape. Apply a child-safe finish, such as clear shellac.

18 **Once dry, remove the tape and glue on the compactor and container.** Attach the back door by inserting the two 2" (5. 1cm) dowels on either side, making sure they are set inside the bevel. Install the lift arms with ¹¹⁄₃₂" (9mm) axle pegs. Attach all the wheels.

SCHOOL BUS

Patterns on pages 136–140

The iconic yellow school bus has always been a reminder of the fun times I had in school. From going on field trips with friends to attending school competitions, I have fond memories of my experiences on the bus. My grandfather drove a bus and would tell me stories about his experiences. I designed school bus to honor him and all those who continue to safely drive kids to school every day.

This project uses yellowheart wood, which can be harder to source than other woods used in the projects so far. Feel free to substitute based on what is available to you.

	Part	Quantity	Materials	Dimensions
PARTS LIST: SCHOOL BUS				
A	Axles	2	Yellowheart, ⁷⁄₃₂" (5.6mm) thick	½" x 4 ¼" (1.3 x 10.8cm)
B	Bumpers	2	Oak, ⅜" (10mm) thick	¾" x 5" (1.9 x 12.7cm)
C	Fenders	2	Yellowheart, ¾" (18mm) thick	2 ¼" x 3" (5.7 x 7.6cm)
D	Back	1	Yellowheart, ½" (12mm) thick	4 ¼" x 4 ¾" (10.8 x 12.1cm)
E	Front	1	Yellowheart, ½" (12mm) thick	3 ½" x 4 ¼" (8.9 x 10.8cm)
F	Bus roof	1	Oak, 1 ¼" (30mm) thick	5 ¼" x 8" (13.3 x 20.3cm)
G	Chassis	1	Yellowheart, ¾" (18mm) thick	4 ¼" x 10 ⅛" (10.8 x 25.7cm)
H	Sides	2	Yellowheart, ½" (12mm) thick	4 ¾" x 7 ½" (12.1 x 19.1cm)
I	Engine	1	Yellowheart, 1 ¾" (4.5cm) thick	3" x 3 ½" (7.6 x 8.9cm)
J	Driver's seat back	1	Oak, ½" (12mm) thick	1 ½" x 1 ¾" (3.8 x 4.4cm)
K	Driver's seat bottom	1	Oak, ¾" (18mm) thick	1 ¼" x 1 ½" (3.2 x 3.8cm)
L	Passenger's seat backs	2	Oak, ½" (12mm) thick	1 ½" x 4" (3.8 x 10.2cm)
M	Passenger's seat bottoms	2	Oak, ¾" (18mm) thick	1 ¼" x 4" (3.2 x 10.2cm)
N	Wheels	4	1 ½" (30mm)-dia.	½" (1.3cm) thick
O	Wheel axle pegs	4	⁷⁄₃₂" (5.6mm) thick	1" (25mm) long
P	Bumper headlights	4	³⁄₁₆" (4mm)-dia.	¾" (18mm) long
Q	Roof headlights	4	⅜" (9mm)-dia.	⅝" (16mm) long

TOOLS & MATERIALS

- Table saw with dado stack
- Scroll saw with #5 and #7 skip-tooth blades
- Drill press with bits: ¼", ⁷⁄₃₂", ³⁄₁₆", and ⅜" (6mm, 5mm, 4mm, and 9mm)
- Router with ¼" (9mm) roundover bit
- Sander with 100 and 150 grit sandpaper
- Miter saw
- Spray adhesive
- White colored pencil (optional)
- Clear packaging tape
- Sandpaper: assorted grits up to 320
- Wood glue
- Child-safe finish, such as clear spray shellac

Woods (see Parts List for exact dimensions)

- Axles: yellowheart, ⁷⁄₃₂" (5.6mm) thick
- Back, front, sides: yellowheart, ½" (12mm) thick
- Fenders, chassis: yellowheart, ¾" (18mm) thick
- Engine: yellowheart, 1 ¾" (4.5cm) thick
- Bumpers: oak, ⅜" (10mm) thick
- Driver's seat bottom, passenger's seat bottom: oak, ¾" (18mm) thick
- Driver's seat back, passenger's seat back: ½" (12mm) thick
- Bus roof: oak, 1 ¼" (30mm) thick
- Wooden axle pegs: ⁷⁄₃₂" (5.6mm)-dia.
- Wooden treaded wheels: 1½" (38mm)-dia.
- Wooden dowels: ³⁄₁₆" (4mm)-dia., ⅜" (9mm)-dia.

1 **Transfer the patterns to the blanks and cut the pieces.** Begin by cutting the chassis to the correct dimensions. Use this to test-fit the other parts. Using clamps, glue up oversized pieces for the engine and the roof. I made my engine blank 8" (203mm) long to safely cut later. I also added an inch to the width of the part to make sure I have plenty to cut off any glue squeeze-out and overhang. Make one of the pieces ¼"–½" (6–13mm) wider. This gives a straight reference edge when ripping to width.

2 **Rip a strip of ½" (13mm) lumber to 4¾" (12.1cm).** Use this to cut blanks for the sides and back. Do not cut the back to length at this time. Cut a ⅛" (3mm)-deep groove ¾" (19mm) wide in each piece. The groove will start ½" (13mm) from the bottom. The chassis will need to have a snug fit in the groove. With the same setup used to cut the groove, cut the ½" (13mm) rabbets on the sides. The ½" (13mm) material should fit flush to the edge of the rabbet.

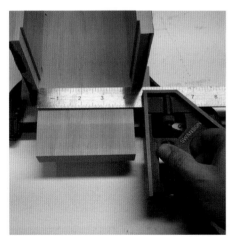
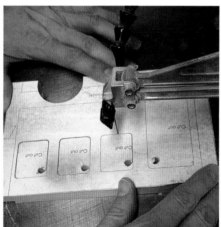

3 **Cut the back and front to length.** These pieces should fit snugly between the two side panels. Clamp the sides to the chassis and measure the exact distance between the rabbets. Cut the front and back to this measurement.

4 **Use painter's tape and spray adhesive to attach the patterns to the sides, back, and front.** Drill pilot holes for the windows and doors. Cut them out using a #5 skip-tooth blade on the scroll saw.

5 **In the chassis, mark where the notches stop.** Dry-fit the sides, back, and front together. Use clamps to keep all parts tight and snug in the grooves. Mark a line where the front sits on the chassis. This will be the minimum length of the notch. The depth of the notch is the thickness of the fenders. I take the fender material and use it as a ruler to mark the line. Cut the notches out using a #7 skip-tooth blade on the scroll saw. It is okay if the notches are a little long because the sides and fenders will cover the area.

6 Cut the engine to the correct width. The width should match the width of the chassis with the cut-out sections. Cut the grooves in the engine. Mark the middle of the engine and set the fence so that the bit or blade is in the center mark. Cut the groove, then move the fence ½" (13mm) back. Cut a groove to the left and right of the center groove. Move the fence back ½" (13mm) again and repeat the process. Cut the angle on the top of the engine. I used a handsaw and then cleaned up the saw marks with a belt sander. Add the profile on the top edges of the engine.

7 Cut and profile the fenders. Rip a piece a little wider than the fenders and about 9" (22.9cm) long out of ¾" (1.9cm) material. Attach or trace the fender pattern to the piece. The back should be along the square edge. Cut the top section of the fenders using a scroll saw, exposing the part that needs to have a ¼" (6mm) roundover profile. Use a ¼" (6mm) roundover bit to profile the fenders. Finish cutting them out using a #7 skip-tooth blade on the scroll saw.

8 Rip the roof blank to the width of the assembled bus. Transfer the pattern to the roof. Mark the location of the holes. Create the dome shape of the roof. This can be done using a table saw with multiple passes and the blade set at multiple angles. Then it can be sanded to the final shape. I used a hand plane to get close to the shape and then sanded to the profile using a belt sander.

TIP

Attach a block of wood to the back of the roof to hold the piece better when sanding. Do this by putting painter's tape on the roof. Then, using CA glue, glue the block to the tape. Clamp until glue is dry. When done, remove the block with a chisel or hammer. This makes an easily removable handle to keep fingers out of the way.

9 **Drill the holes for the lights in the roof.** Use a brad point or Forstner bit to drill the holes in the roof ⅜" (9mm) deep. Sand the roof with 100-grit sandpaper to remove any pencil and sanding marks. Finish sanding using 150-grit sandpaper and break any sharp edges and corners. Cut ⅜" (9mm) wood dowels ⅝" (16mm) long. Glue and insert the dowels in the holes.

10 **Make the seats and benches.** Rip a piece of ¾" (19mm) lumber (I used walnut) 1¼" (32mm) wide and about 12" (305mm) long. Cut a ½" (13mm) rabbet ¼" (6mm) deep. Then, put a ¼" (6mm) roundover on the same face as the rabbet. Rip a ½" (13mm)-thick piece of lumber 1¾" (45mm) wide and about 12" (305mm) long. Round over the top of the piece with a ¼" (6mm) roundover bit. You will need to use a fence on the router because the bushing will not work when the piece is flipped over to profile the other side.

11 **Cut the driver seat back and bottom to length.** Rip the remaining seat back to 1½" (38mm). Cut the bench pieces to length. Glue the seat backs and bottoms together. Clamp and let dry. After they are dry, use 100-grit sandpaper to clean up any glue squeeze-out and break any sharp edges. Sand with 150-grit sandpaper.

12 **Remove all patterns and sand the parts.** Start at 100 grit and then move to 150 grit. Break all edges on the windows. Clamp the driver side window and back to the chassis. Glue the seats in place. The bench seats should be against the side. They are spaced about 1" (25mm) apart. The driver's seat goes next to the window, about ¼" (6mm) away from the side. Clamp the seats in place and let the glue dry.

13 **Glue the sides, back, and front to the chassis.** I would recommend doing a dry run without glue first, because there are many parts and several clamps. Allow the glue to dry, then sand any glue squeeze-out.

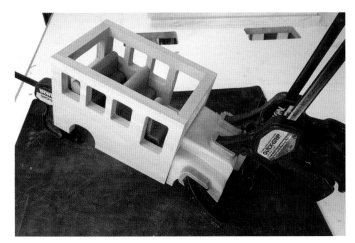

14 **Glue the engine and fenders to the chassis.** They will be against the front and flush to the bottom of the side panel.

15 **Attach the wheels.** Rip two pieces that are ½" (13mm) thick that are 1¼" (32mm) wide and 4¼" (10.8cm) long. These will be used to attach the wheels. Mark and drill 7⁄32" (5mm) holes 1" (25mm) deep on both ends on the part. Dry-fit wheels on the axles. Use the wheels on the axles to align and glue the axles on the chassis. When the wheels are centered in the wheel hubs, clamp them into place and let dry.

16 **Attach the bumpers.** Rip a ¾" (19mm) thick piece to ⅜" (9mm) wide. Cut the bumpers from this piece. Mark and drill 3⁄16" (4mm) holes in the bumpers. Attach the bumpers to the front and back of the bus. Using the holes as guides, drill 3⁄16" (4mm) holes ¾" (19mm) deep. Cut the dowels and glue and insert them in the holes. Cut off the excess and sand smooth.

17 **Sand all parts with 150-grit sandpaper.** Soften all edges and corners. Prepare the bus for finishing by taping off the gluing area for the roof. This is to prevent this area from finishing because glue does not bond well with finish. Finish using a child-safe finish.

18 **After the finish has dried, remove the tape and glue the top to the bus.** Glue the wheels on the bus with axle pegs.

Patterns

TUGBOAT

See parts list on page 32 for precise dimensions

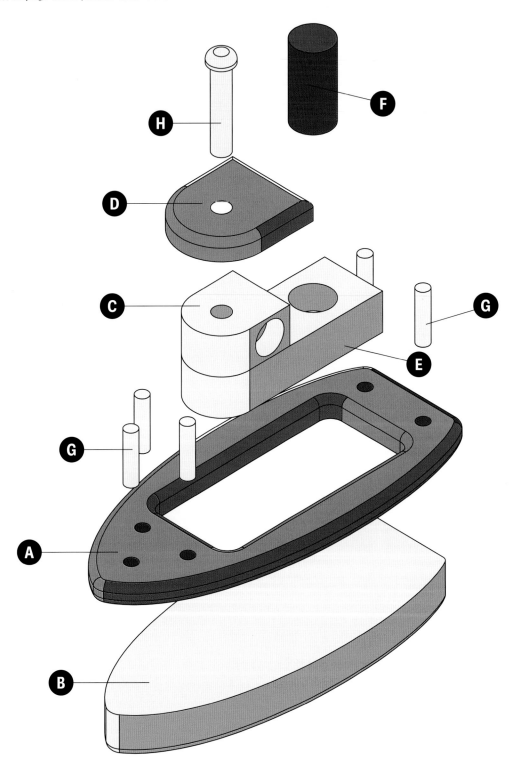

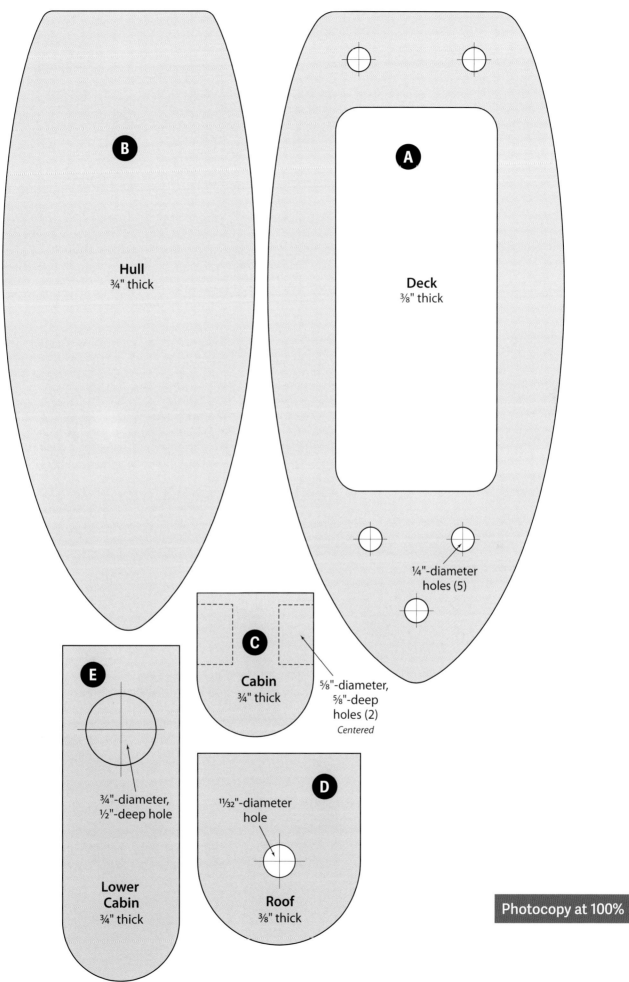

Hull
¾" thick

Deck
⅜" thick

¼"-diameter
holes (5)

C

Cabin
¾" thick

⅝"-diameter,
⅝"-deep
holes (2)
Centered

E

¾"-diameter,
½"-deep hole

**Lower
Cabin**
¾" thick

D

¹¹⁄₃₂"-diameter
hole

Roof
⅜" thick

Photocopy at 100%

CITY CARS

See parts list on page 36 for precise dimensions

Photocopy at 100%

• Mini

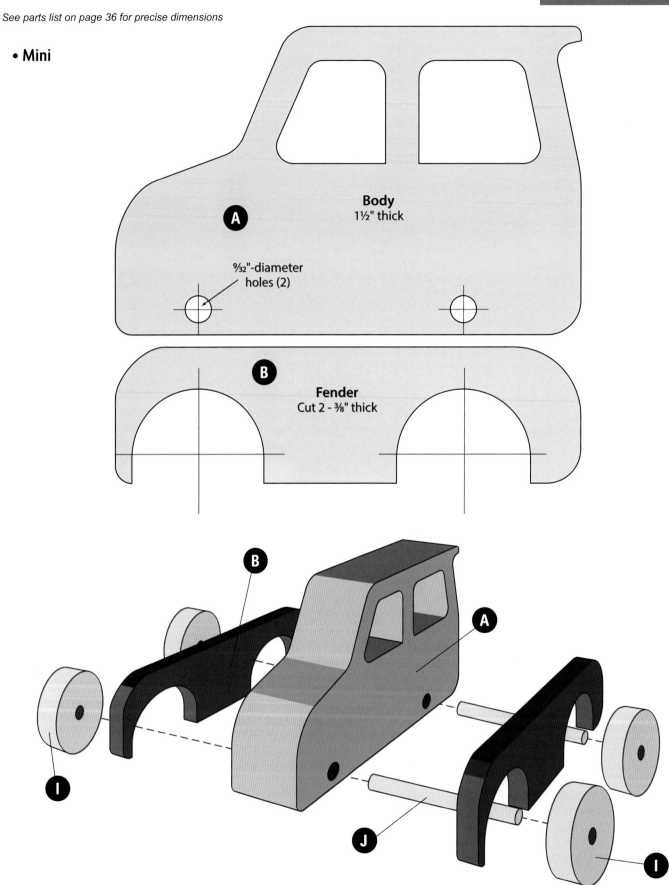

Body
1½" thick

A

⁹⁄₃₂"-diameter
holes (2)

B

Fender
Cut 2 - ⅜" thick

• Sports Car

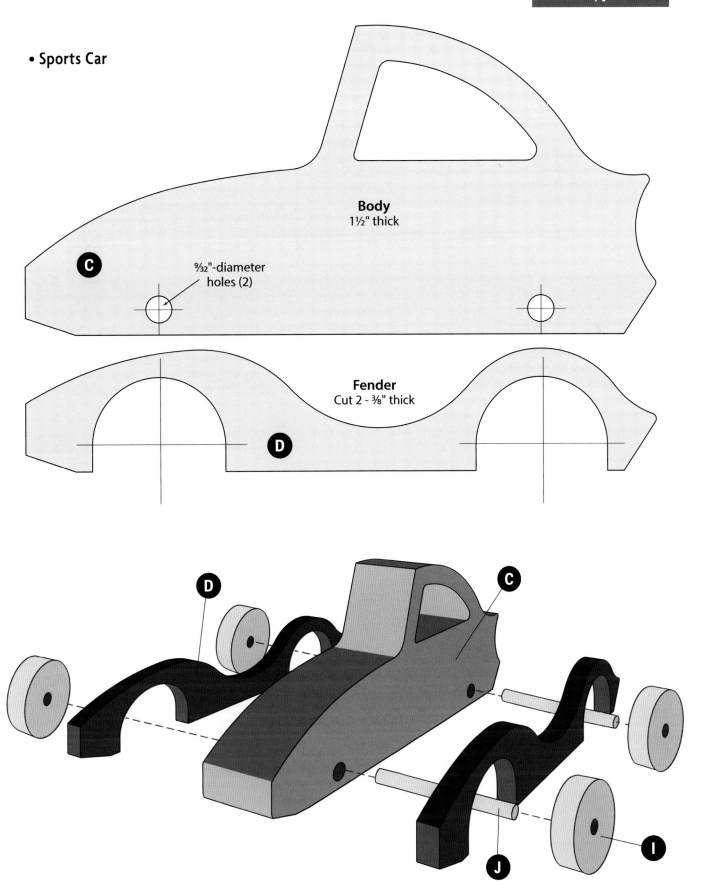

Body
1½" thick

⁹⁄₃₂"-diameter
holes (2)

Fender
Cut 2 - ⅜" thick

CITY CARS

See parts list on page 36 for precise dimensions

Photocopy at 100%

• Bug

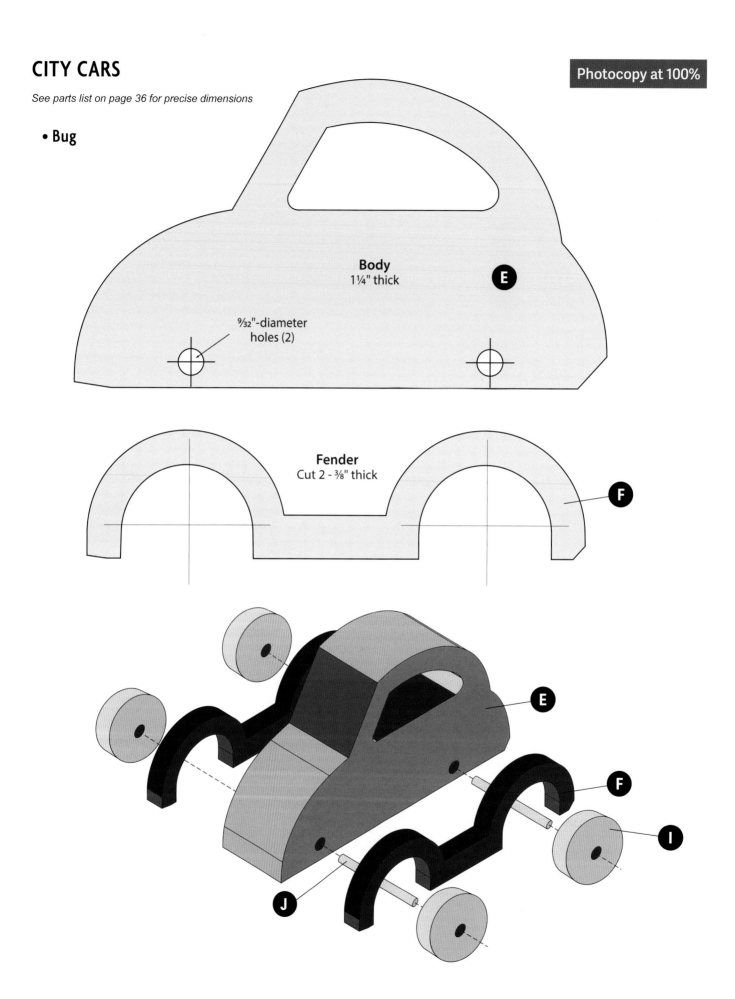

Body
1¼" thick

E

⁹⁄₃₂"-diameter
holes (2)

Fender
Cut 2 - ⅜" thick

F

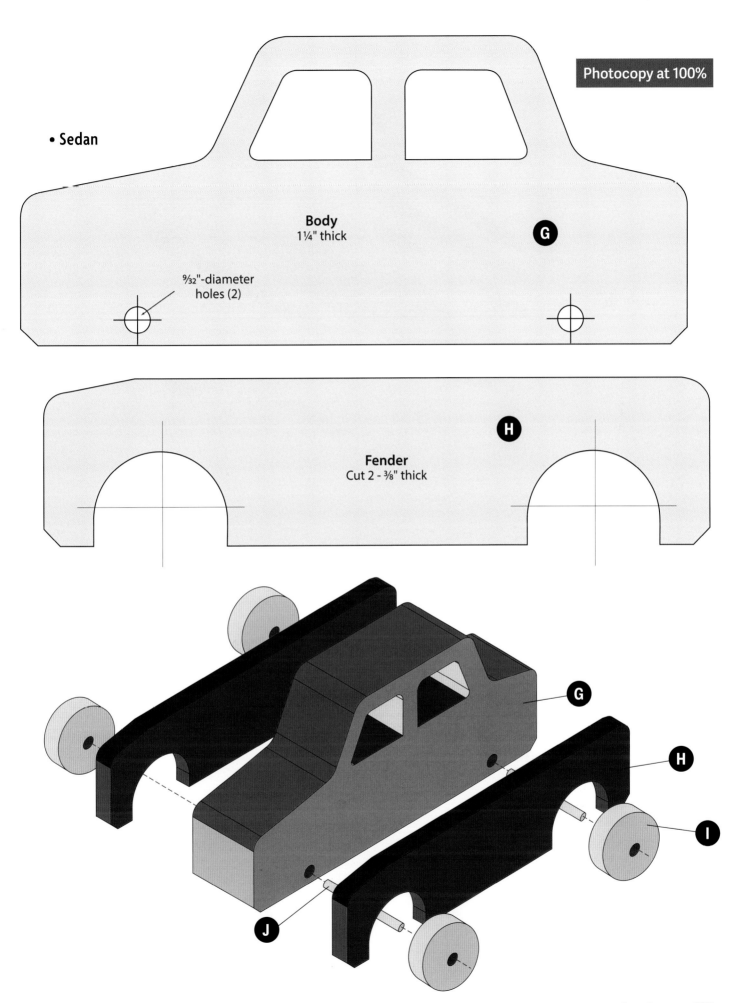

• Sedan

Body
1¼" thick

G

⁹⁄₃₂"-diameter
holes (2)

H

Fender
Cut 2 - ³⁄₈" thick

G

H

I

J

FIGHTER JET

See parts list on page 40 for precise dimensions

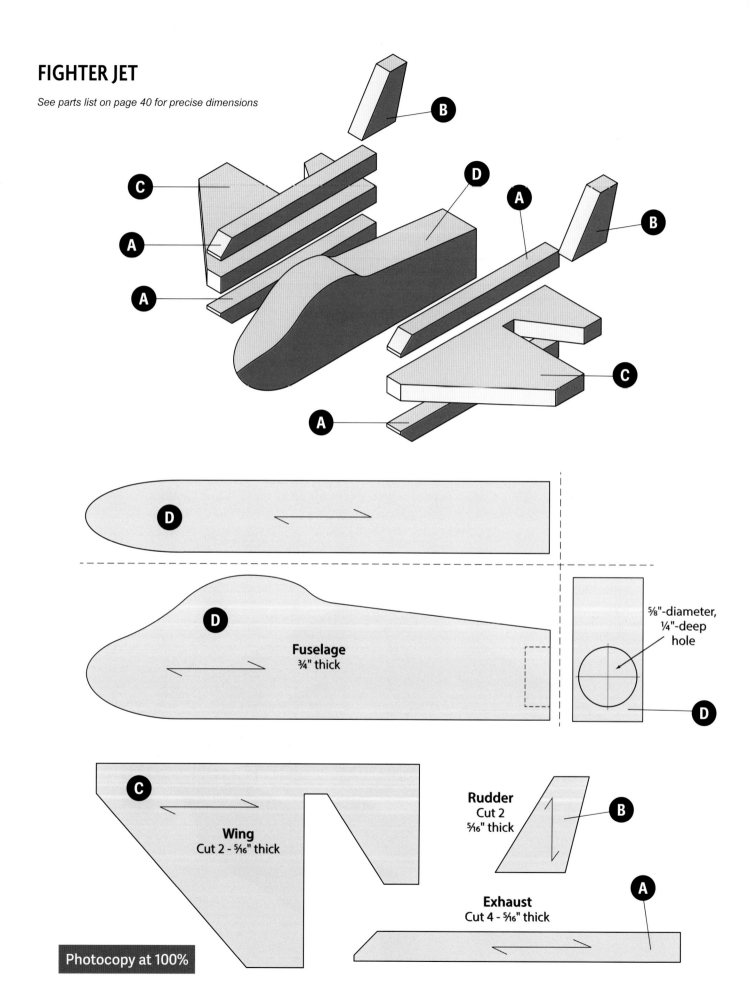

Fuselage
¾" thick

⅝"-diameter,
¼"-deep
hole

Wing
Cut 2 - ⁵⁄₁₆" thick

Rudder
Cut 2
⁵⁄₁₆" thick

Exhaust
Cut 4 - ⁵⁄₁₆" thick

Photocopy at 100%

RACE CAR

See parts list on page 52 for precise dimensions

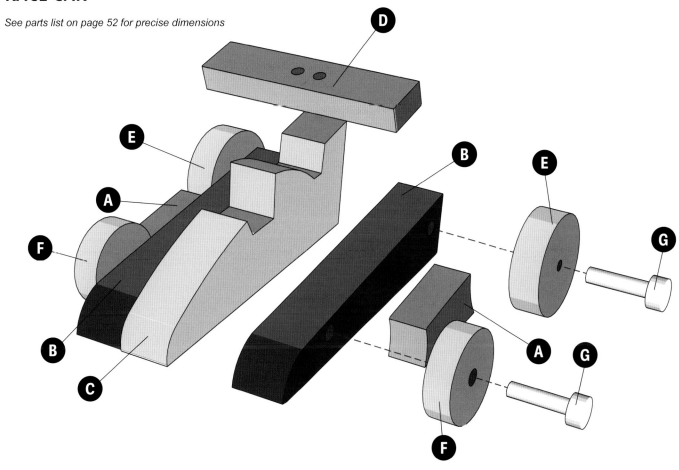

Photocopy at 100%

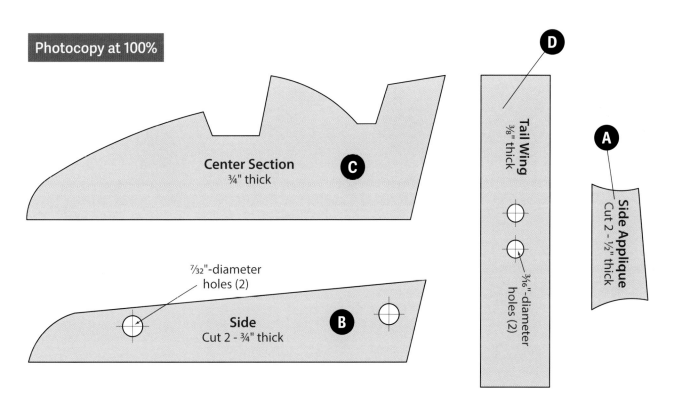

Center Section
¾" thick

Tail Wing
⅜" thick

³⁄₁₆"-diameter
holes (2)

Side Applique
Cut 2 - ½" thick

⁷⁄₃₂"-diameter
holes (2)

Side
Cut 2 - ¾" thick

MODEL T

See parts list on page 44 for precise dimensions

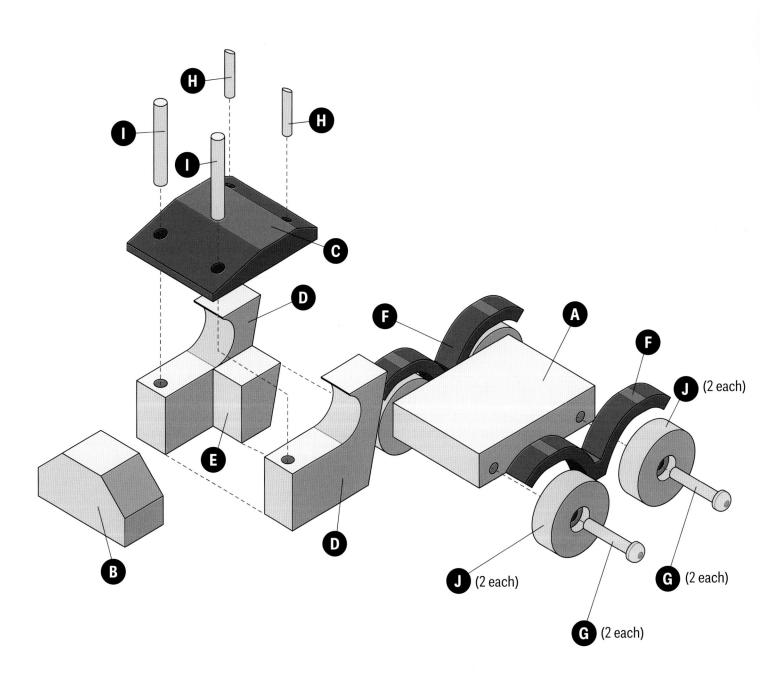

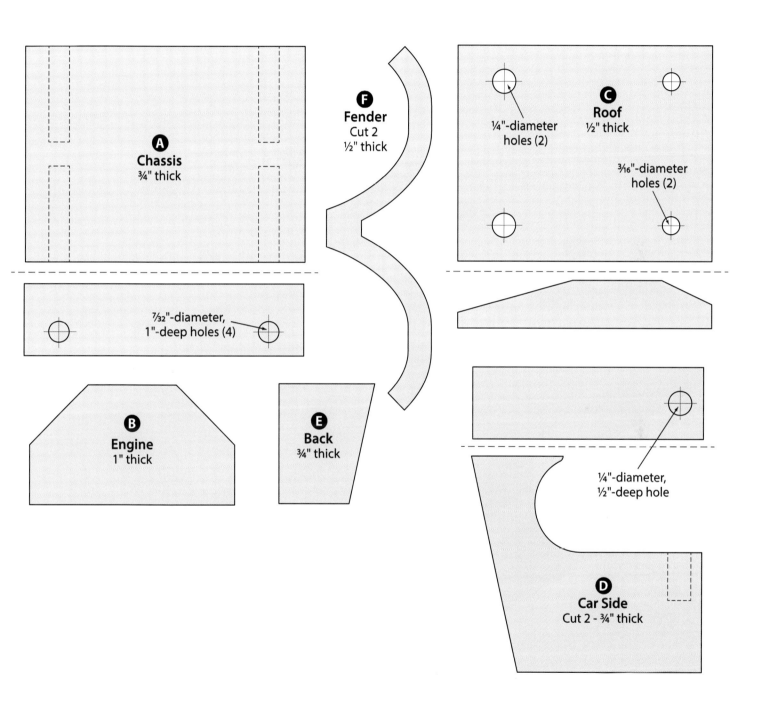

F
Fender
Cut 2
½" thick

A
Chassis
¾" thick

C
Roof
½" thick

¼"-diameter
holes (2)

³⁄₁₆"-diameter
holes (2)

⁷⁄₃₂"-diameter,
1"-deep holes (4)

B
Engine
1" thick

E
Back
¾" thick

¼"-diameter,
½"-deep hole

D
Car Side
Cut 2 - ¾" thick

JEEP

See parts list on page 48 for precise dimensions

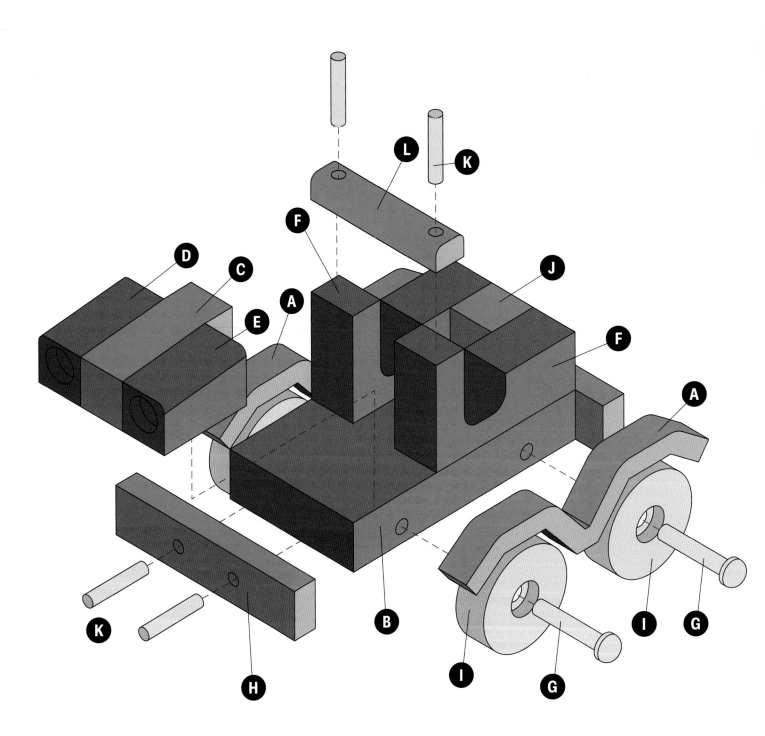

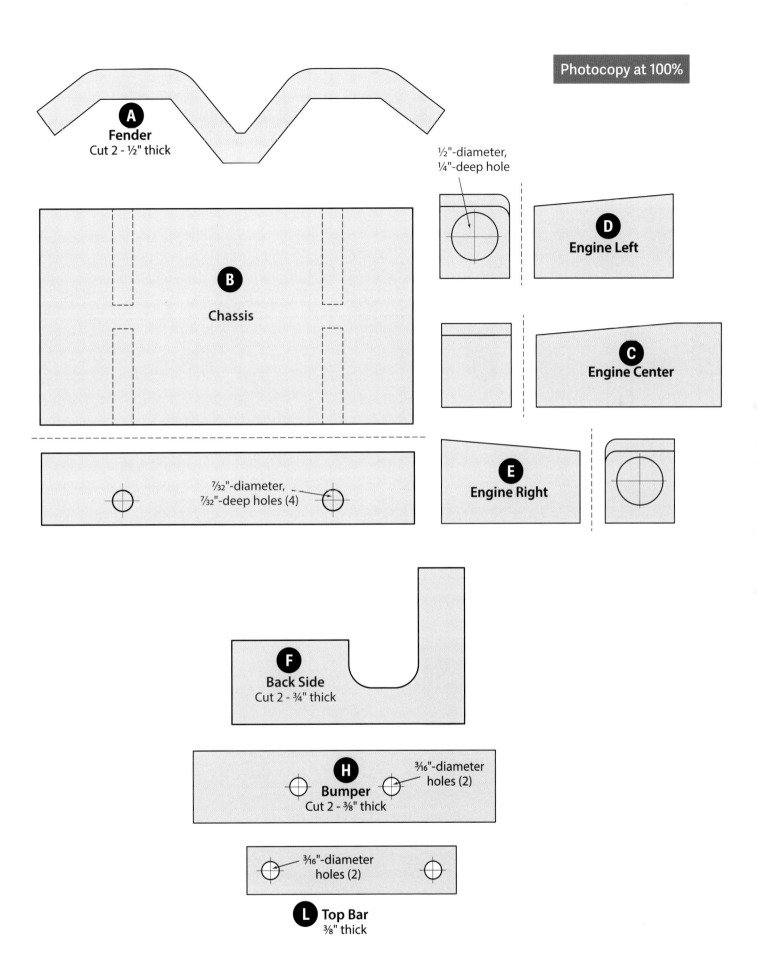

A
Fender
Cut 2 - ½" thick

½"-diameter,
¼"-deep hole

B
Chassis

D
Engine Left

C
Engine Center

E
Engine Right

⁷⁄₃₂"-diameter,
⁷⁄₃₂"-deep holes (4)

F
Back Side
Cut 2 - ¾" thick

H
Bumper
Cut 2 - ⅜" thick

³⁄₁₆"-diameter
holes (2)

³⁄₁₆"-diameter
holes (2)

L **Top Bar**
⅜" thick

FLATBED TRUCK

See parts list on page 56 for precise dimensions

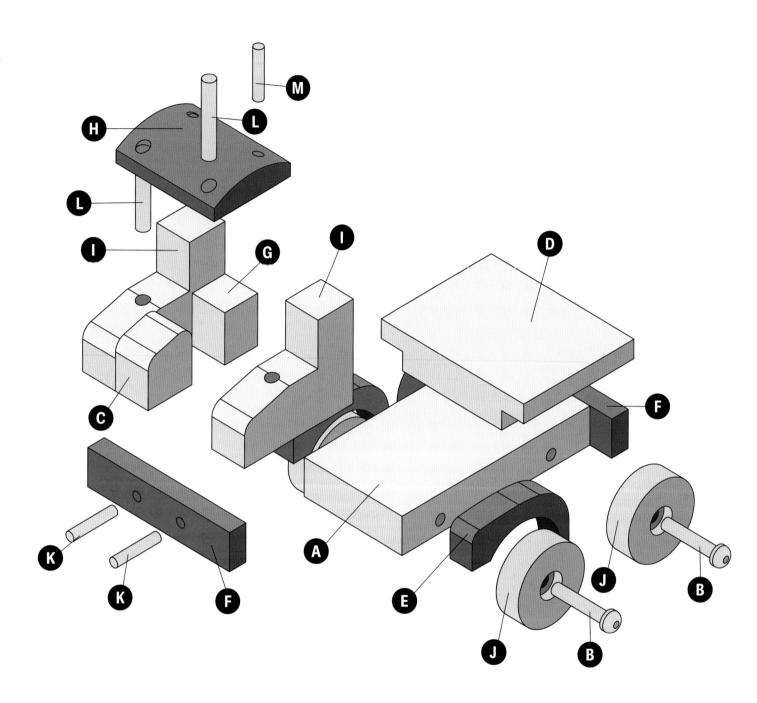

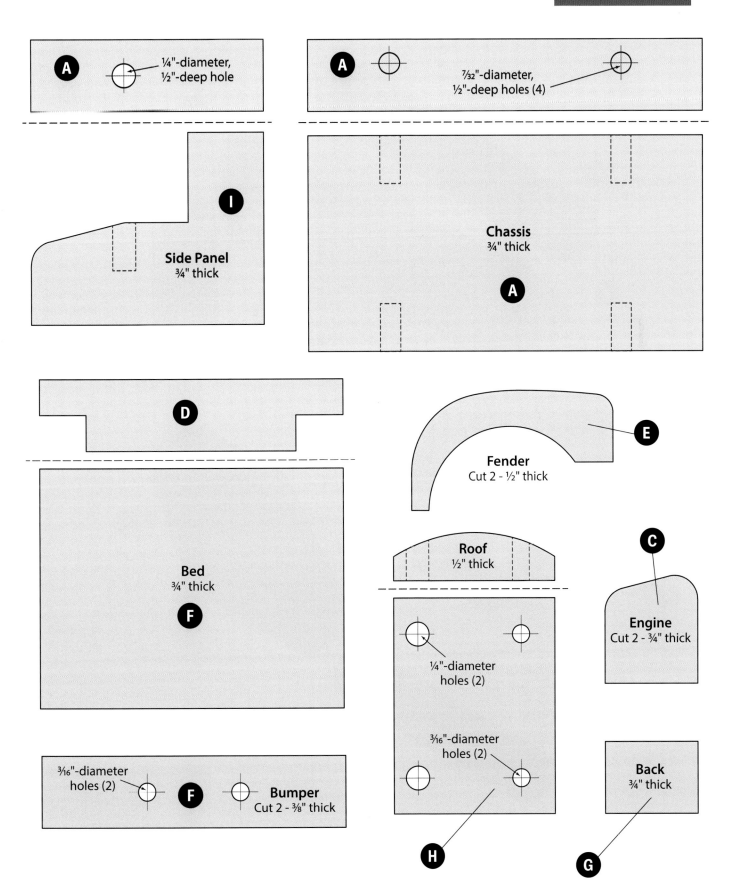

A

¼"-diameter,
½"-deep hole

A

⁷⁄₃₂"-diameter,
½"-deep holes (4)

I

Side Panel
¾" thick

Chassis
¾" thick

A

D

Fender
Cut 2 - ½" thick

E

Bed
¾" thick

F

Roof
½" thick

C

Engine
Cut 2 - ¾" thick

¼"-diameter
holes (2)

³⁄₁₆"-diameter
holes (2)

³⁄₁₆"-diameter
holes (2)

F

Bumper
Cut 2 - ⅜" thick

H

Back
¾" thick

G

HELICOPTER

See parts list on page 60 for precise dimensions

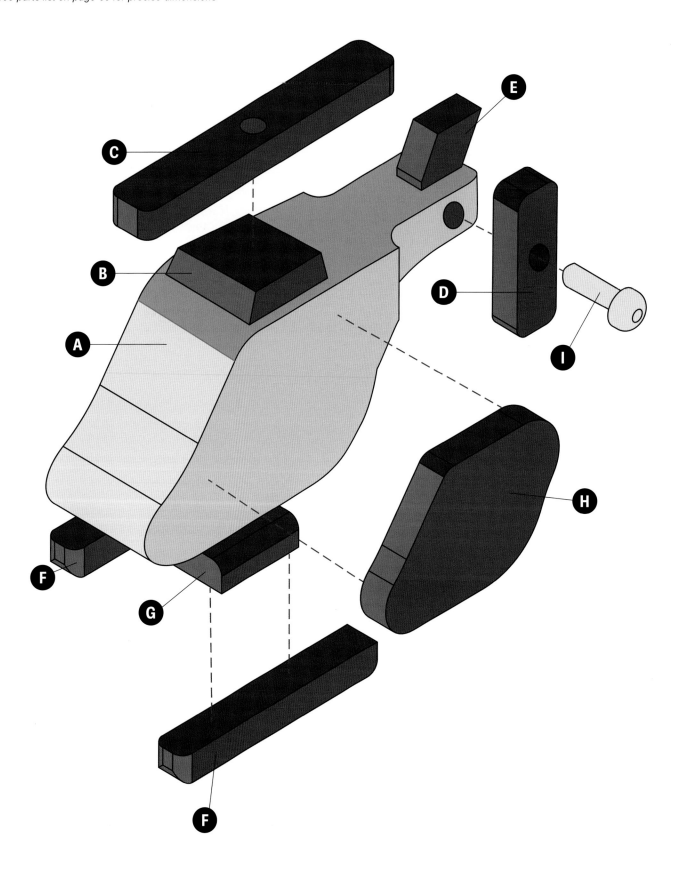

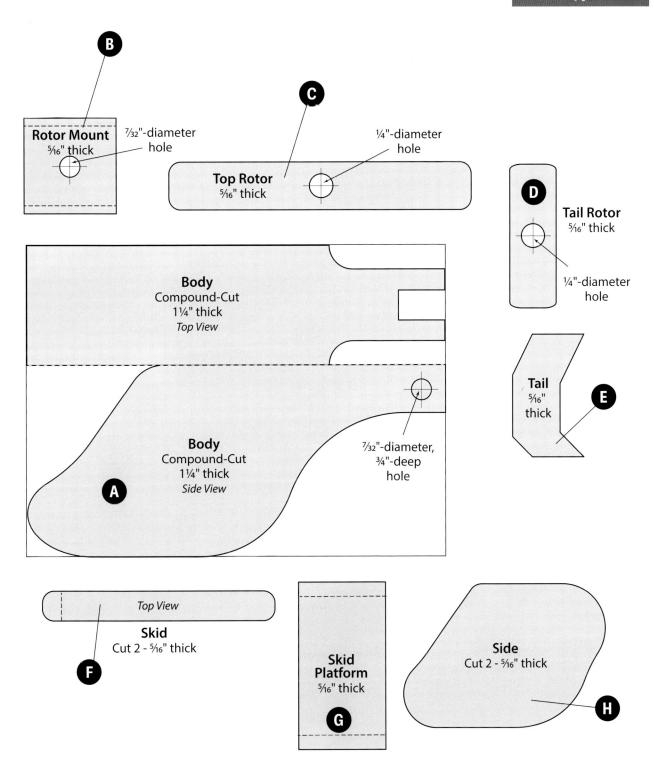

B
Rotor Mount
⁵⁄₁₆" thick
⁷⁄₃₂"-diameter hole

C
Top Rotor
⁵⁄₁₆" thick
¼"-diameter hole

D
Tail Rotor
⁵⁄₁₆" thick
¼"-diameter hole

Body
Compound-Cut
1¼" thick
Top View

Body
Compound-Cut
1¼" thick
Side View
A

⁷⁄₃₂"-diameter, ¾"-deep hole

Tail
⁵⁄₁₆" thick
E

Top View
Skid
Cut 2 - ⁵⁄₁₆" thick
F

Skid Platform
⁵⁄₁₆" thick
G

Side
Cut 2 - ⁵⁄₁₆" thick
H

BIPLANE

See parts list on page 64 for precise dimensions

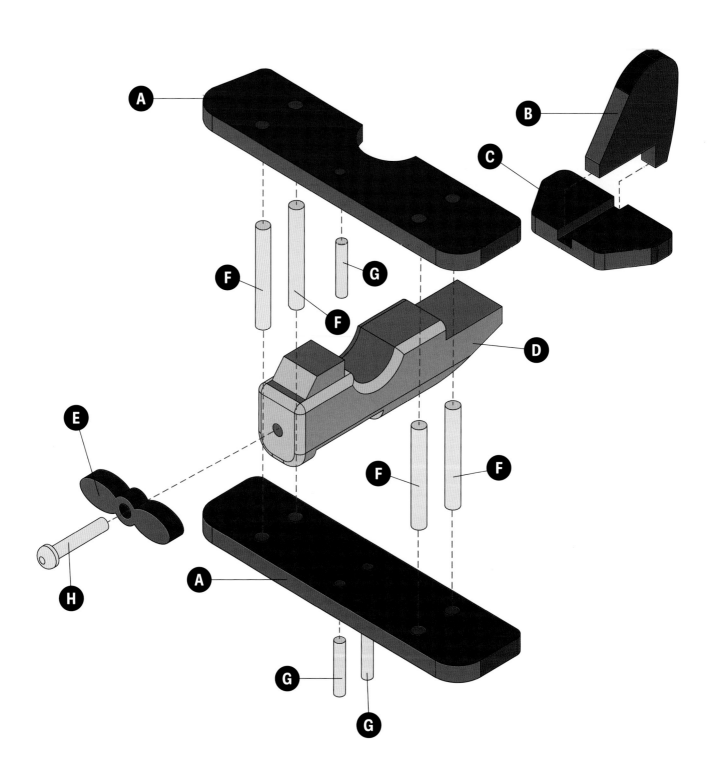

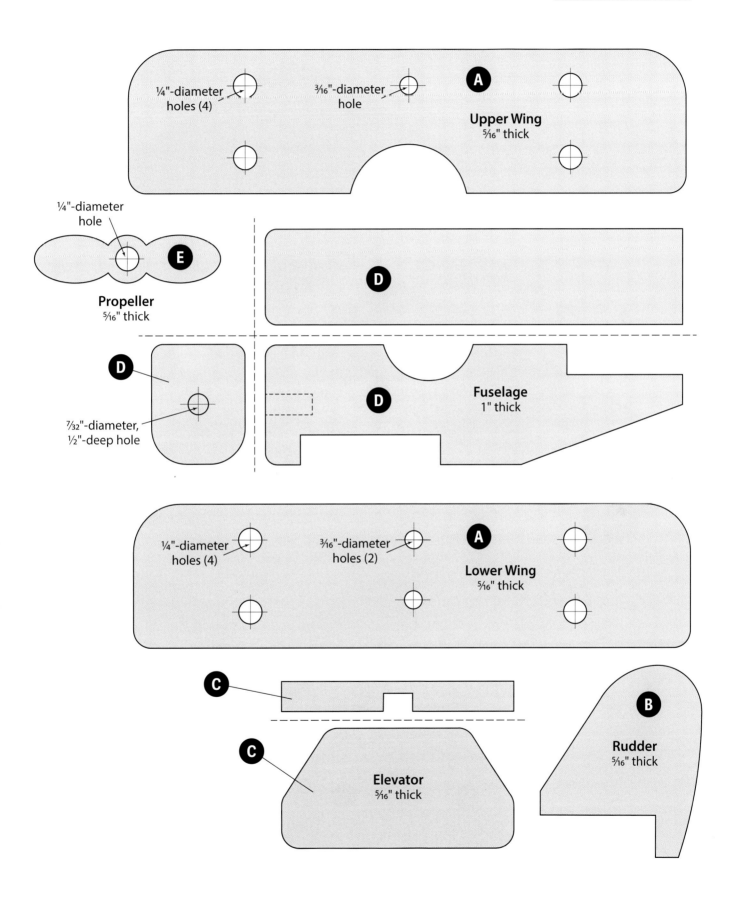

¼"-diameter holes (4)

³⁄₁₆"-diameter hole

A

Upper Wing
⁵⁄₁₆" thick

¼"-diameter hole

E

Propeller
⁵⁄₁₆" thick

D

D

⁷⁄₃₂"-diameter, ½"-deep hole

D

Fuselage
1" thick

¼"-diameter holes (4)

³⁄₁₆"-diameter holes (2)

A

Lower Wing
⁵⁄₁₆" thick

C

C

Elevator
⁵⁄₁₆" thick

B

Rudder
⁵⁄₁₆" thick

GOLF CART

See parts list on page 70 for precise dimensions

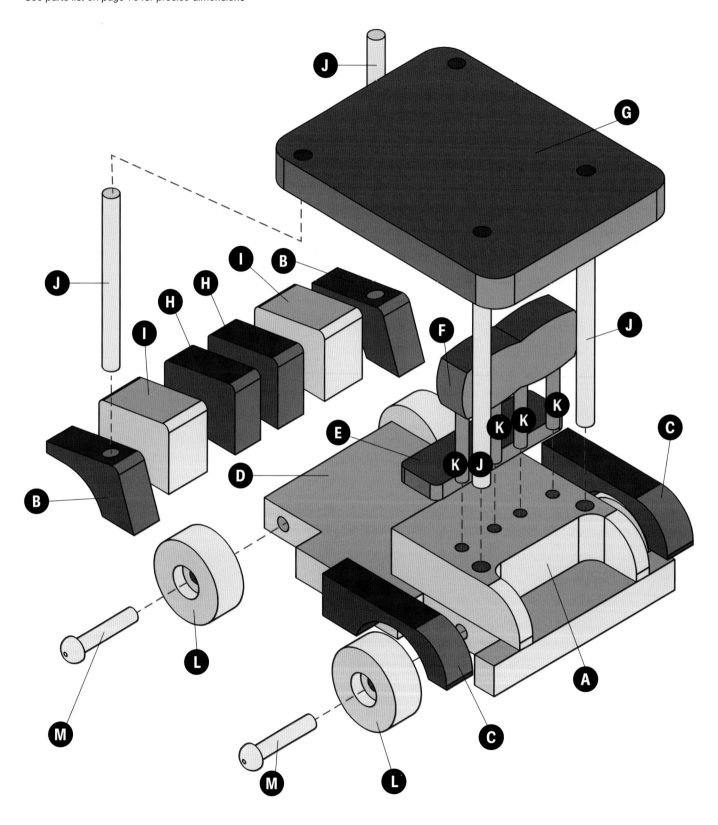

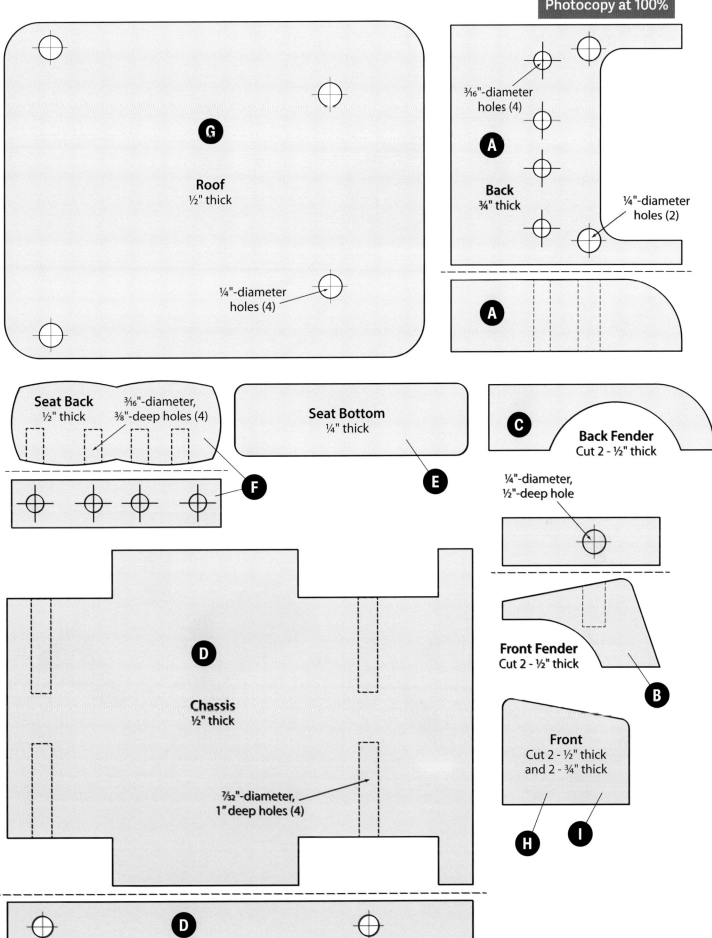

G

Roof
½" thick

¼"-diameter
holes (4)

³⁄₁₆"-diameter
holes (4)

A

Back
¾" thick

¼"-diameter
holes (2)

A

Seat Back
½" thick

³⁄₁₆"-diameter,
⅜"-deep holes (4)

F

Seat Bottom
¼" thick

E

C

Back Fender
Cut 2 - ½" thick

¼"-diameter,
½"-deep hole

Front Fender
Cut 2 - ½" thick

B

D

Chassis
½" thick

⁷⁄₃₂"-diameter,
1" deep holes (4)

Front
Cut 2 - ½" thick
and 2 - ¾" thick

H

I

D

SKID LOADER

See parts list on page 74 for precise dimensions

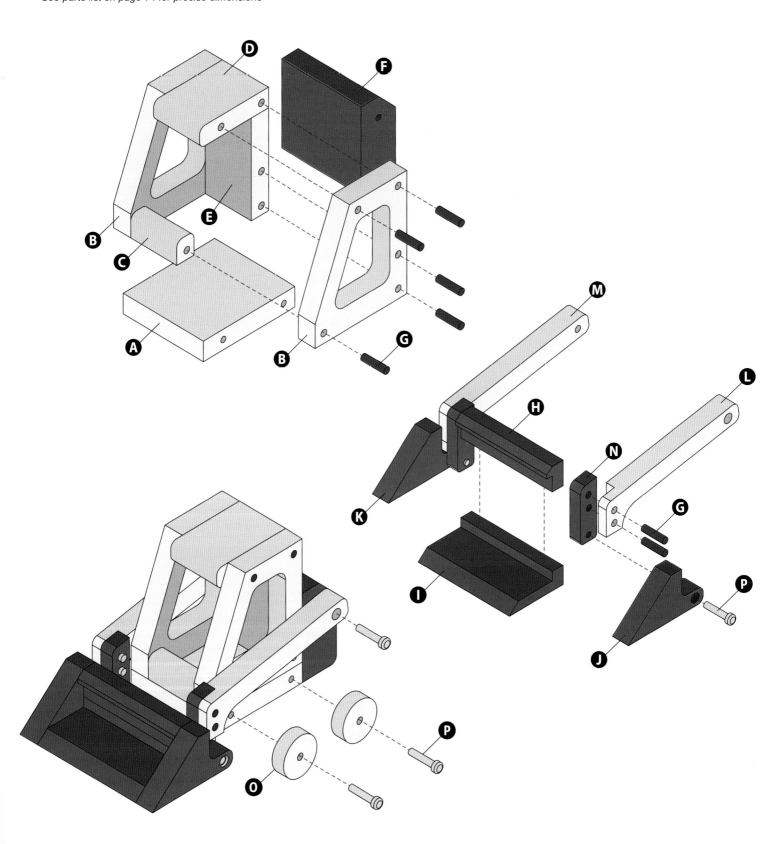

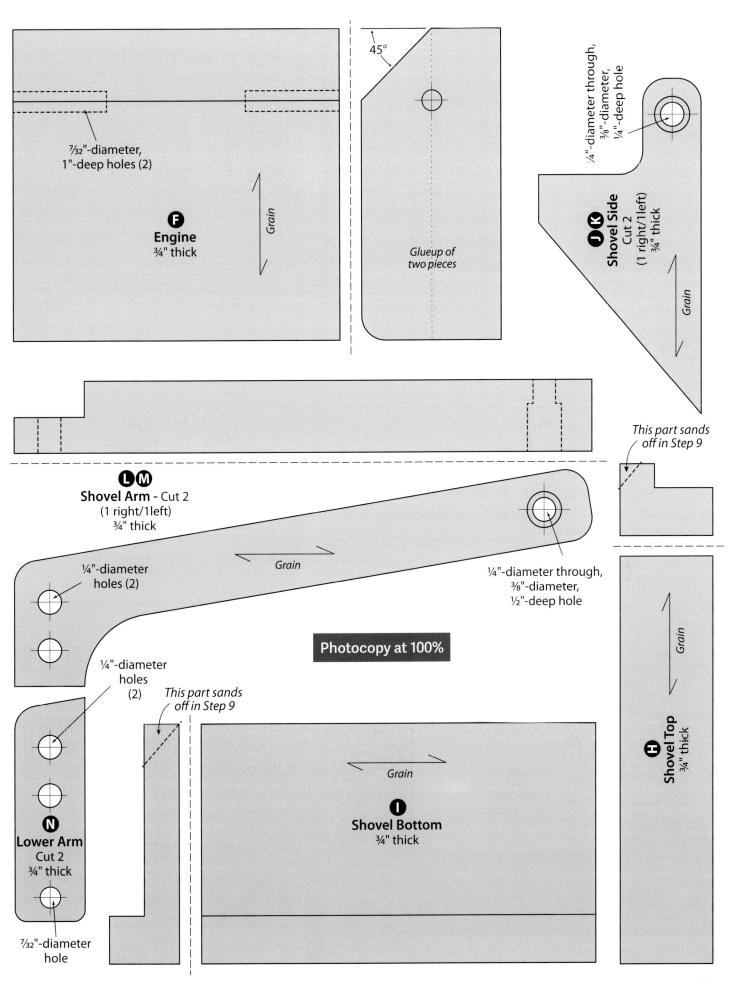

7/32"-diameter,
1"-deep holes (2)

F
Engine
¾" thick

Grain

45°

*Glueup of
two pieces*

¼"-diameter through,
⅜"-diameter,
¼"-deep hole

J K
Shovel Side
Cut 2
(1 right/1left)
¾" thick

Grain

*This part sands
off in Step 9*

L M
Shovel Arm - Cut 2
(1 right/1left)
¾" thick

Grain

¼"-diameter
holes (2)

¼"-diameter through,
⅜"-diameter,
½"-deep hole

Photocopy at 100%

¼"-diameter
holes
(2)

*This part sands
off in Step 9*

Grain

I
Shovel Bottom
¾" thick

Grain

H
Shovel Top
¾" thick

N
Lower Arm
Cut 2
¾" thick

7/32"-diameter
hole

Photocopy at 100%

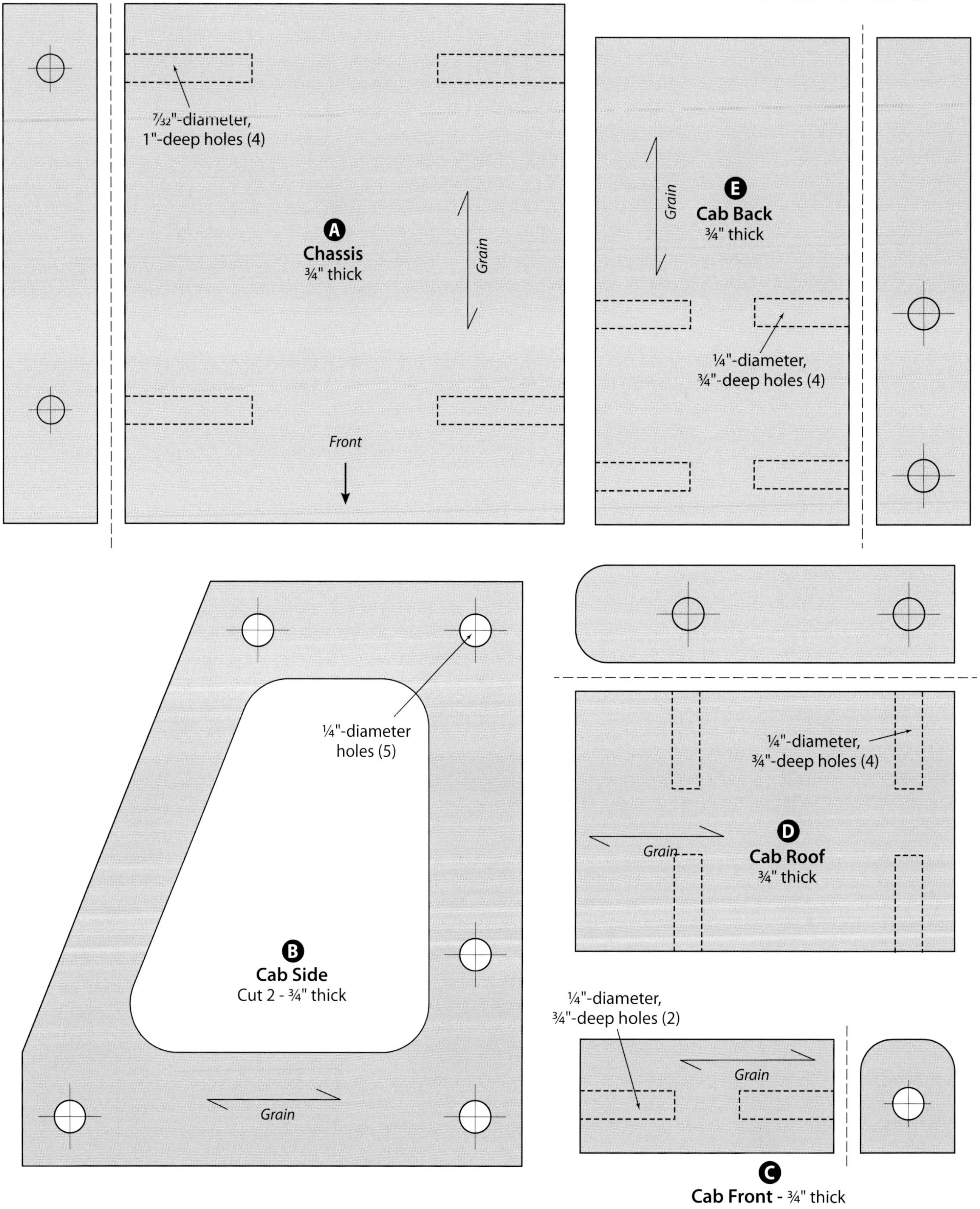
7/32"-diameter,
1"-deep holes (4)
A
Chassis
3/4" thick
Grain
Front
E
Cab Back
3/4" thick
Grain
1/4"-diameter,
3/4"-deep holes (4)
1/4"-diameter
holes (5)
B
Cab Side
Cut 2 - 3/4" thick
Grain
1/4"-diameter,
3/4"-deep holes (4)
D
Cab Roof
3/4" thick
Grain
1/4"-diameter,
3/4"-deep holes (2)
Grain
C
Cab Front - 3/4" thick

TOW TRUCK

See parts list on page 78 for precise dimensions

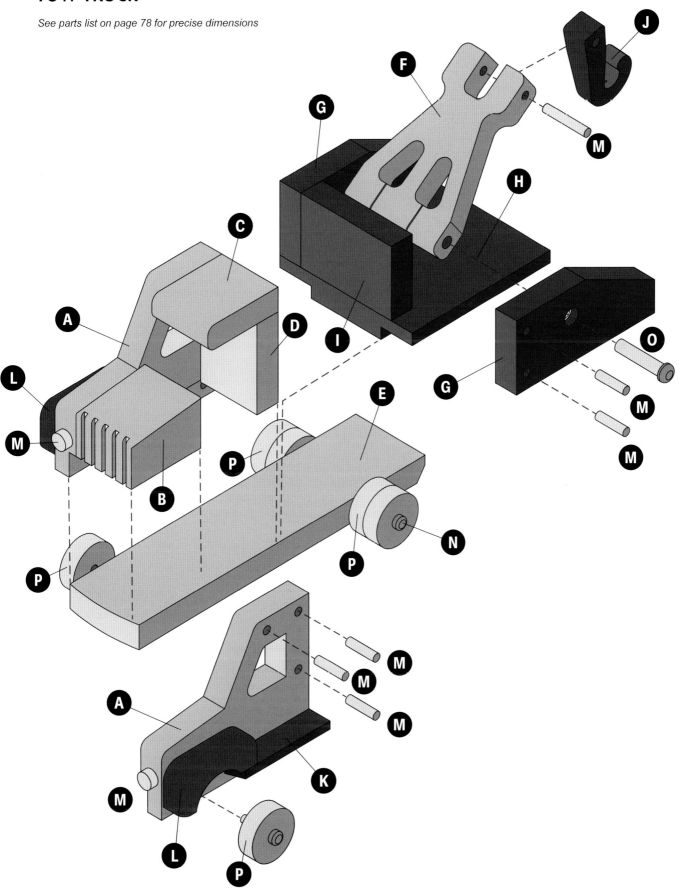

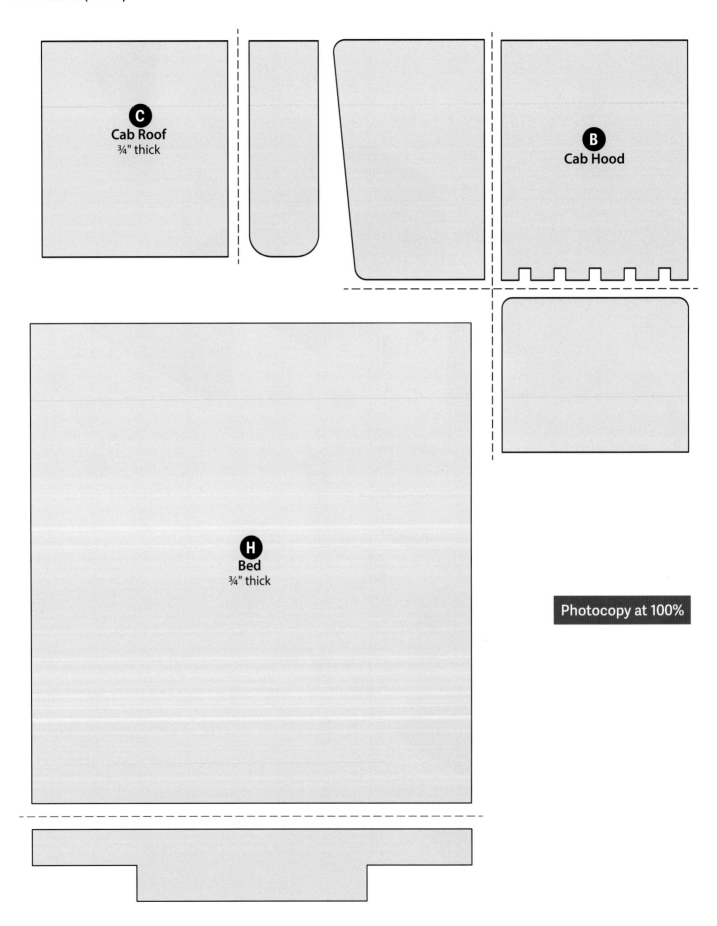

C
Cab Roof
¾" thick

B
Cab Hood

H
Bed
¾" thick

Photocopy at 100%

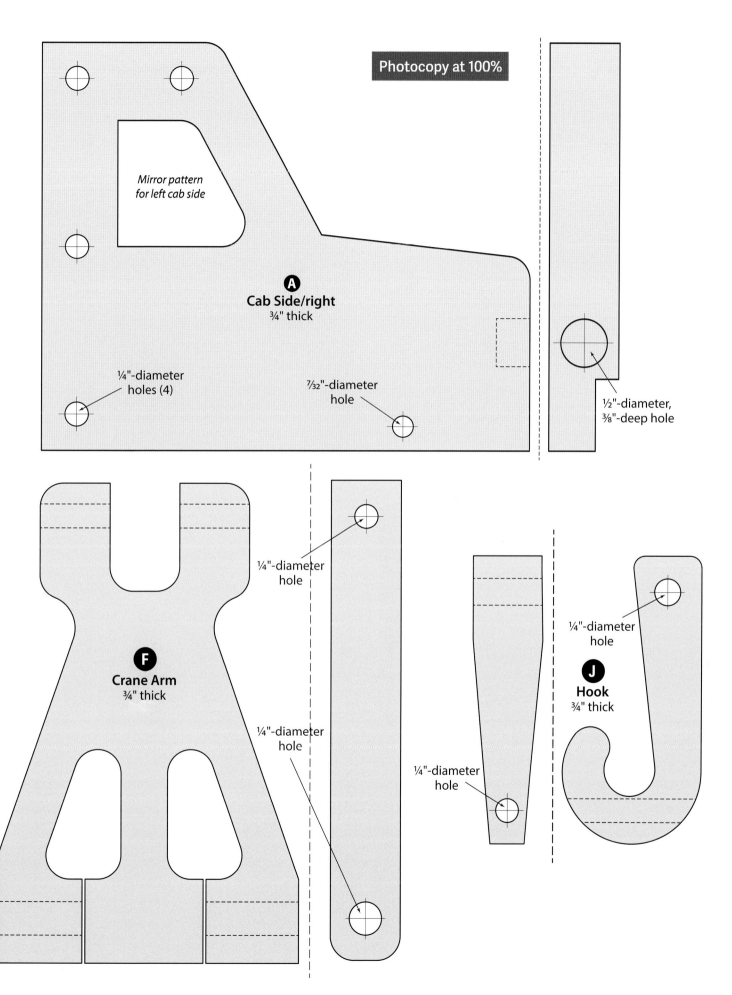

Photocopy at 100%

Mirror pattern for left cab side

A
Cab Side/right
¾" thick

¼"-diameter holes (4)

⁷⁄₃₂"-diameter hole

½"-diameter, ⅜"-deep hole

¼"-diameter hole

¼"-diameter hole

F
Crane Arm
¾" thick

¼"-diameter hole

J
Hook
¾" thick

¼"-diameter hole

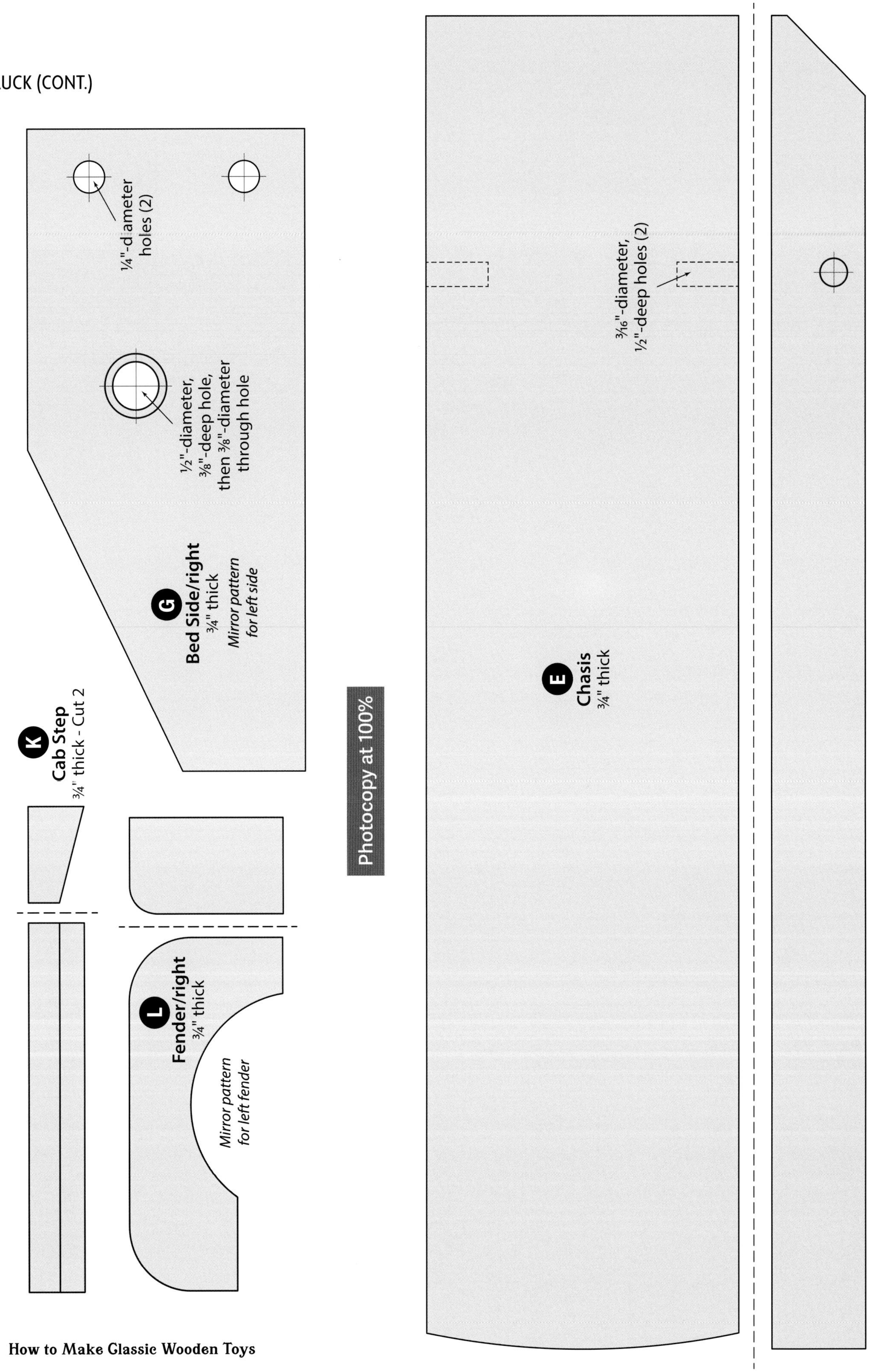

¼"-diameter holes (2)

½"-diameter, ⅜"-deep hole, then ⅜"-diameter through hole

G

Bed Side/right
¾" thick

Mirror pattern for left side

K

Cab Step
¾" thick – Cut 2

Photocopy at 100%

L

Fender/right
¾" thick

Mirror pattern for left fender

³⁄₁₆"-diameter, ½"-deep holes (2)

E

Chasis
¾" thick

TRACTOR

See parts list on page 84 for precise dimensions

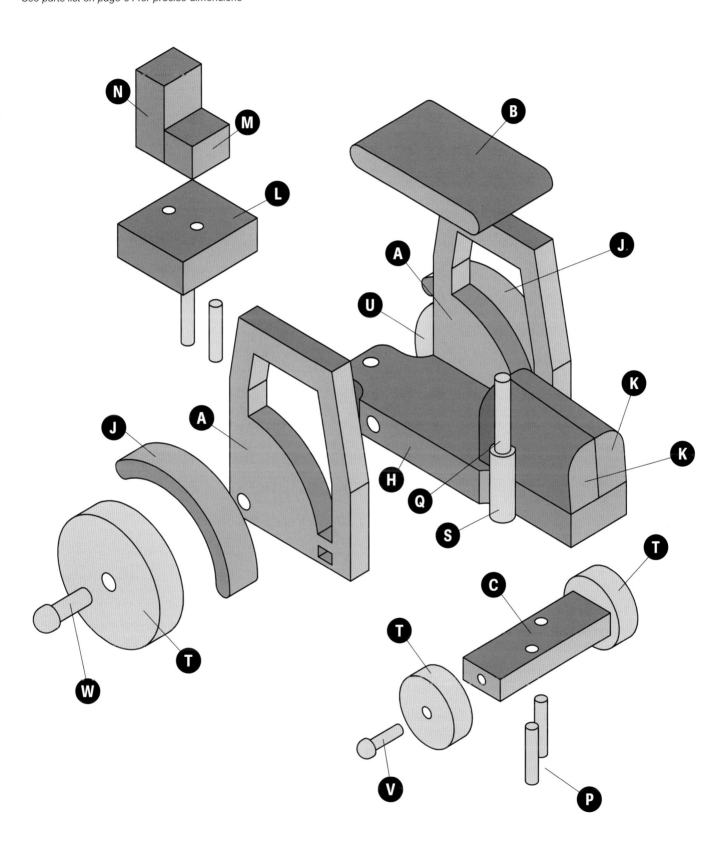

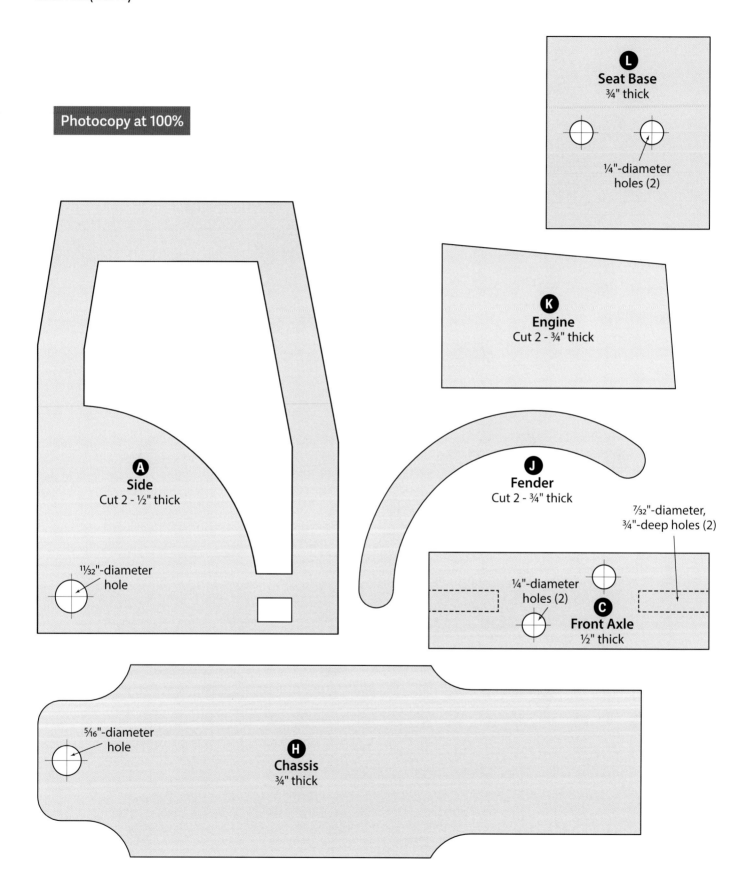

Photocopy at 100%

L
Seat Base
¾" thick

¼"-diameter
holes (2)

K
Engine
Cut 2 - ¾" thick

A
Side
Cut 2 - ½" thick

1¹⁄₃₂"-diameter
hole

J
Fender
Cut 2 - ¾" thick

⁷⁄₃₂"-diameter,
¾"-deep holes (2)

¼"-diameter
holes (2)

C
Front Axle
½" thick

⁵⁄₁₆"-diameter
hole

H
Chassis
¾" thick

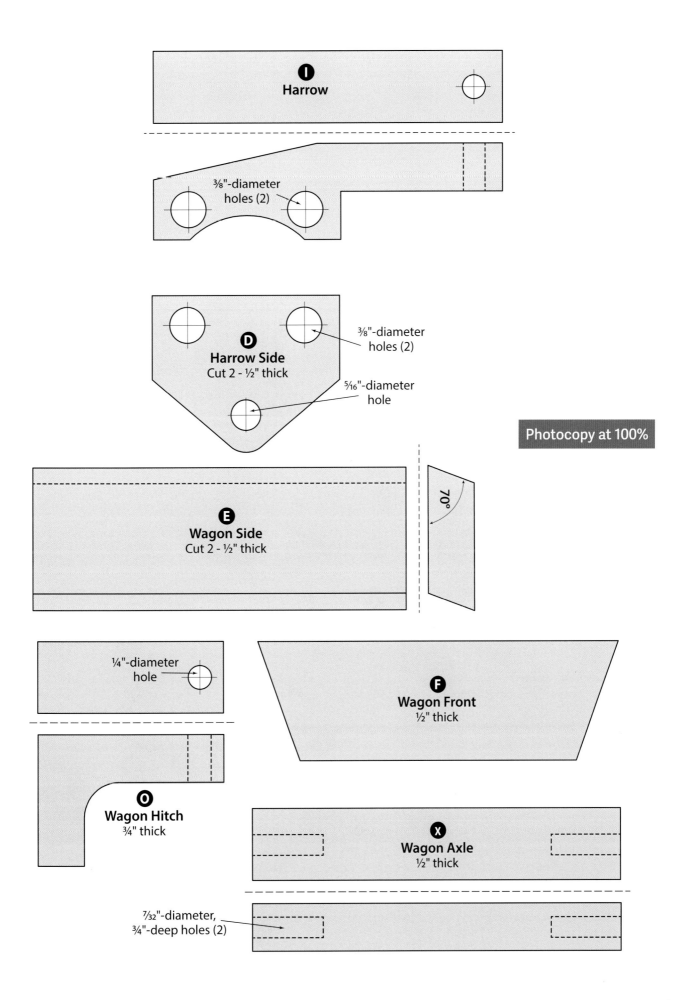

I

Harrow

⅜"-diameter
holes (2)

⅜"-diameter
holes (2)

D

Harrow Side
Cut 2 - ½" thick

⁵⁄₁₆"-diameter
hole

Photocopy at 100%

E

Wagon Side
Cut 2 - ½" thick

70°

¼"-diameter
hole

F

Wagon Front
½" thick

O

Wagon Hitch
¾" thick

X

Wagon Axle
½" thick

⁷⁄₃₂"-diameter,
¾"-deep holes (2)

GARBAGE TRUCK

See parts list on page 90 for precise dimensions

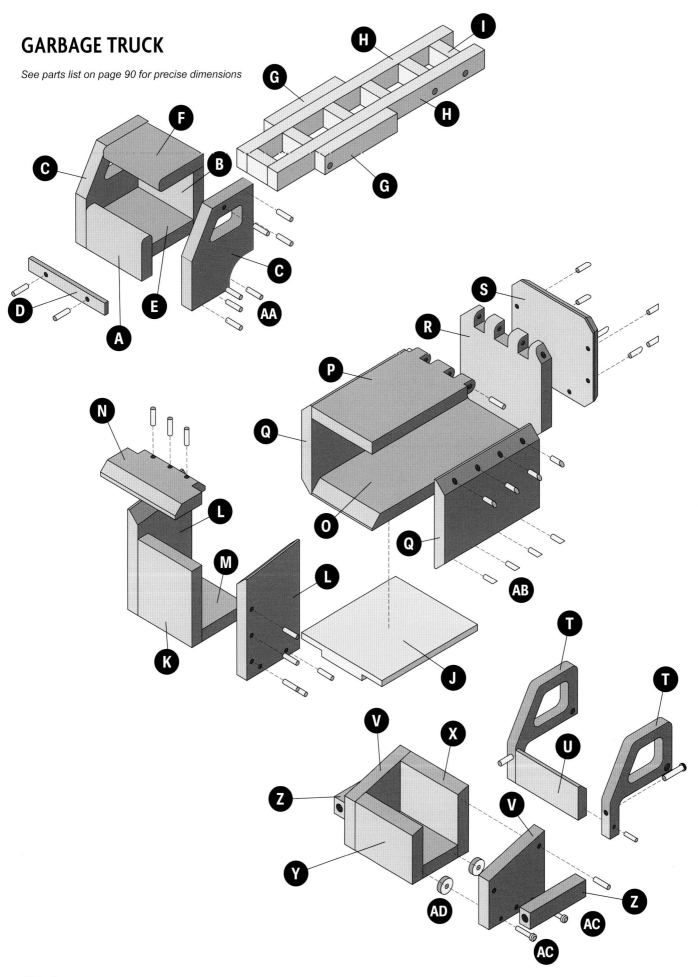

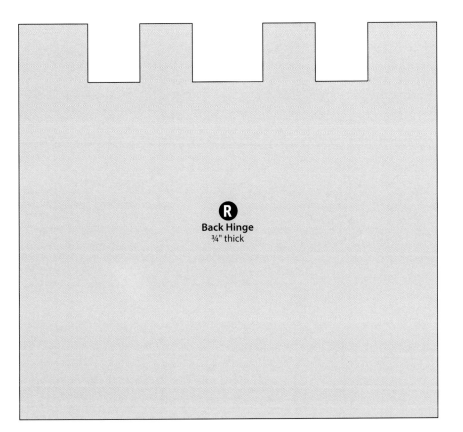

¼"-diameter
hole

*Side
view*

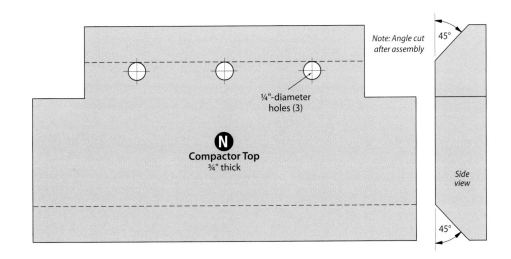

*Note: Angle cut
after assembly*

45°

¼"-diameter
holes (3)

N
Compactor Top
¾" thick

45°

*Side
view*

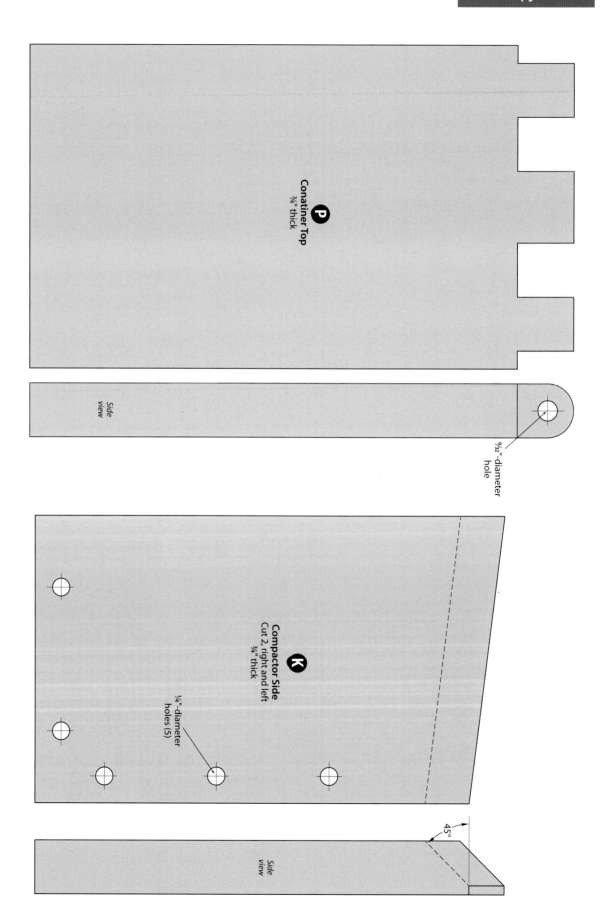

P

Conatiner Top
¾" thick

Side
view

⁹⁄₃₂"-diameter
hole

K

Compactor Side
Cut 2, right and left
¾" thick

¼"-diameter
holes (5)

45°

Side
view

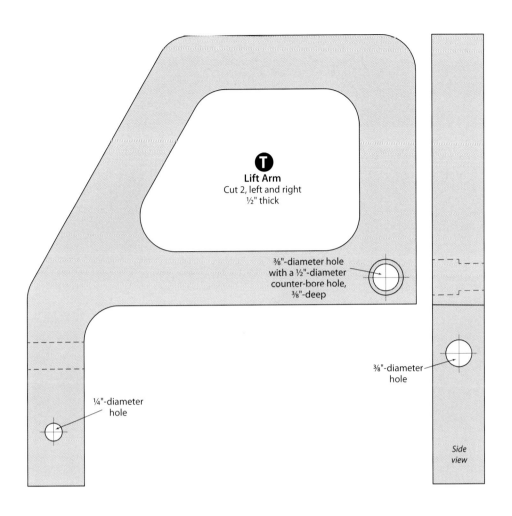

Lift Arm
Cut 2, left and right
½" thick

⅜"-diameter hole
with a ½"-diameter
counter-bore hole,
⅜"-deep

¼"-diameter
hole

⅜"-diameter
hole

*Side
view*

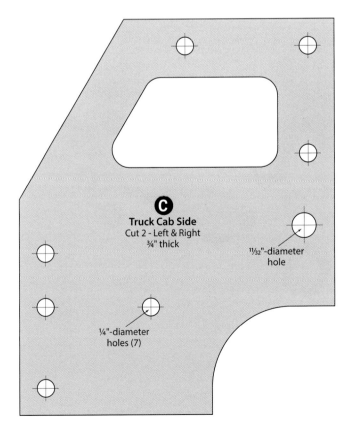

Truck Cab Side
Cut 2 - Left & Right
¾" thick

¹¹/₃₂"-diameter
hole

¼"-diameter
holes (7)

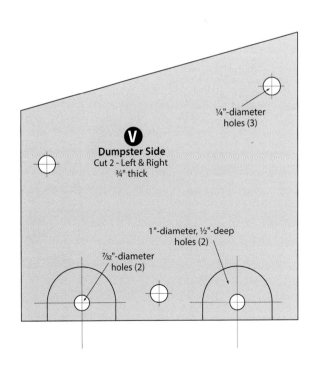

Dumpster Side
Cut 2 - Left & Right
¾" thick

¼"-diameter
holes (3)

1"-diameter, ½"-deep
holes (2)

⁷/₃₂"-diameter
holes (2)

SCHOOL BUS

See parts list on page 96 for precise dimensions

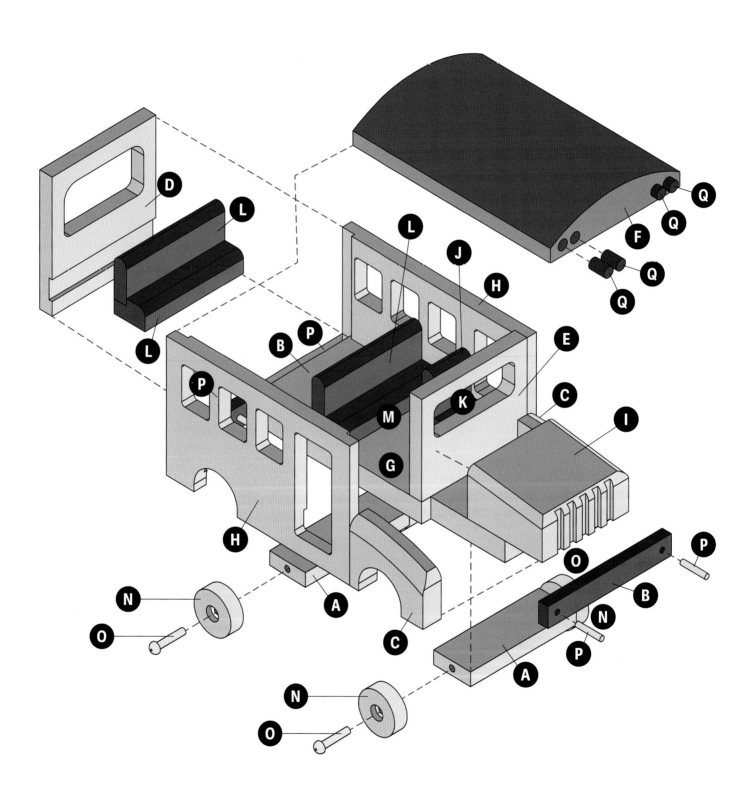

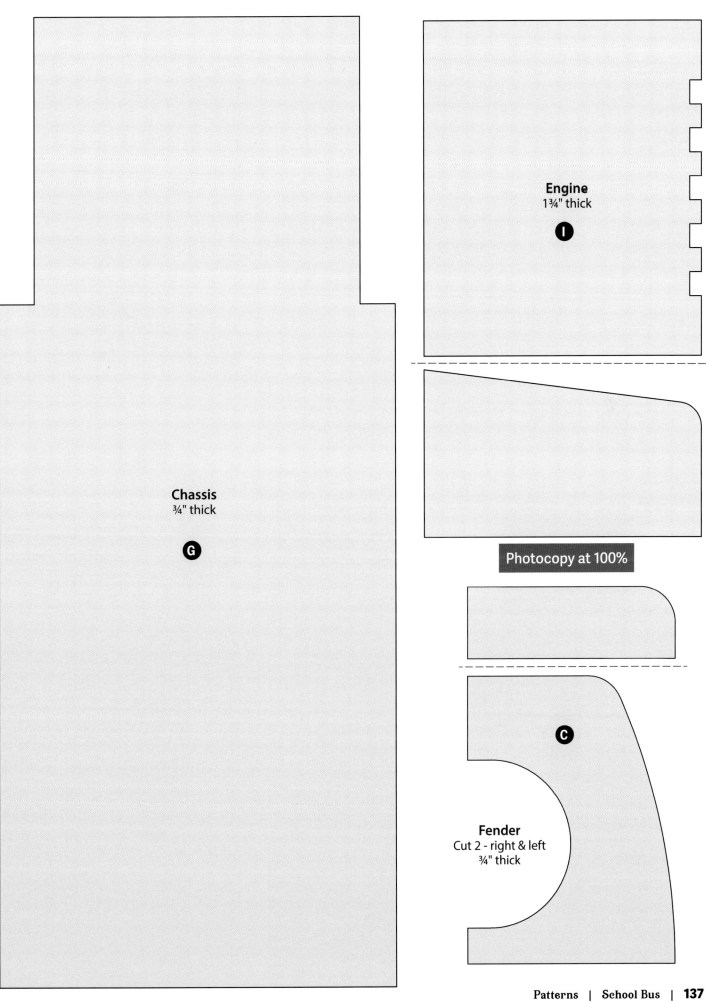

Chassis
¾" thick

G

Engine
1¾" thick

I

Photocopy at 100%

C

Fender
Cut 2 - right & left
¾" thick

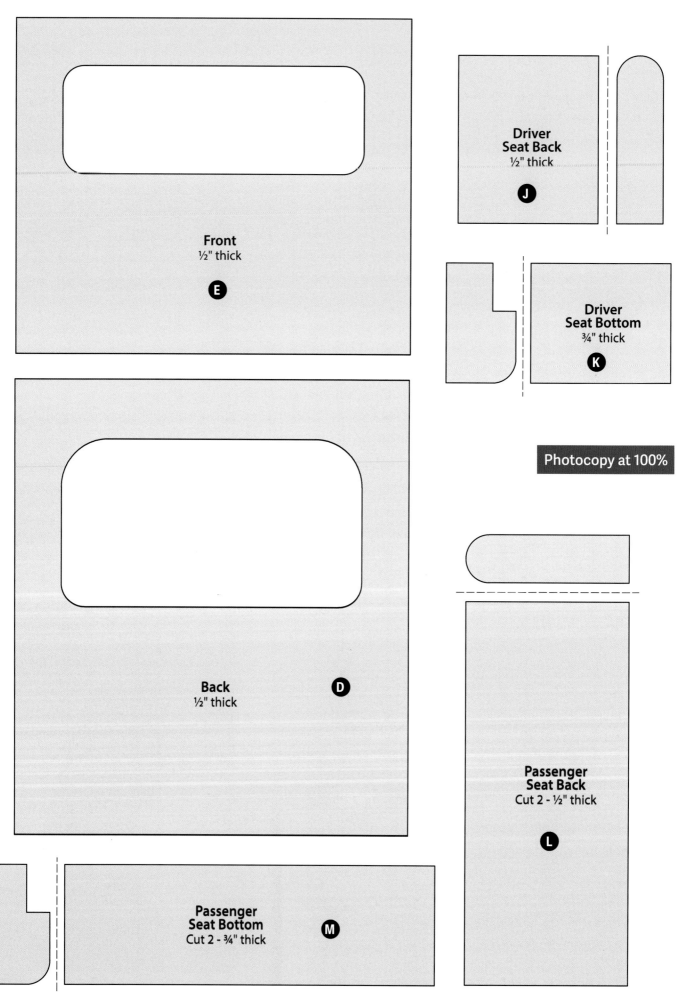

Front
½" thick

E

**Driver
Seat Back**
½" thick

J

**Driver
Seat Bottom**
¾" thick

K

Photocopy at 100%

Back
½" thick

D

**Passenger
Seat Back**
Cut 2 - ½" thick

L

**Passenger
Seat Bottom**
Cut 2 - ¾" thick

M

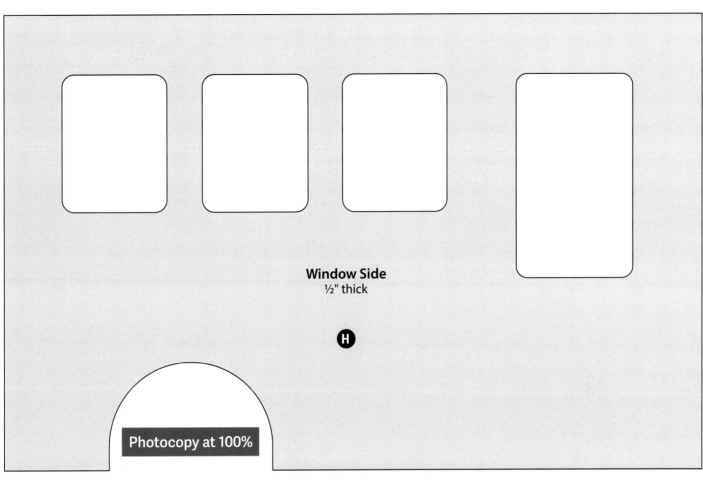

Window Side
½" thick

H

Photocopy at 100%

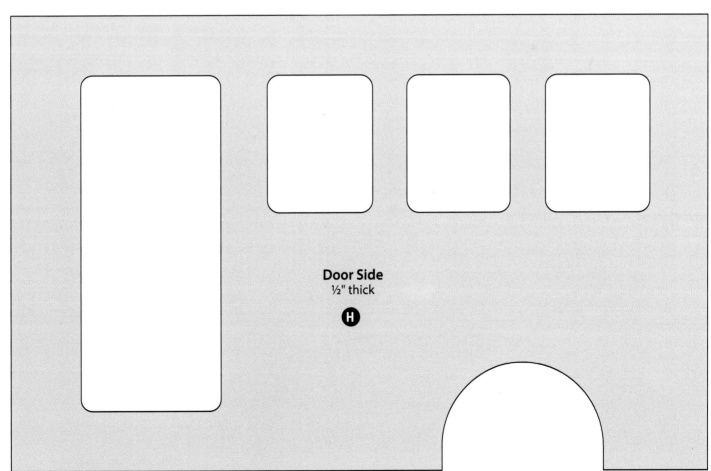

Door Side
½" thick

H

F

Bus Roof
1¼" thick

Axle
Cut 2 - ½" thick

A

⁷⁄₃₂"-diameter holes (2)

Bumper
Cut 2 - ⅜" thick

B

³⁄₁₆"-diameter holes (2)

⅜"-diameter, ⅜"-deep holes (4)

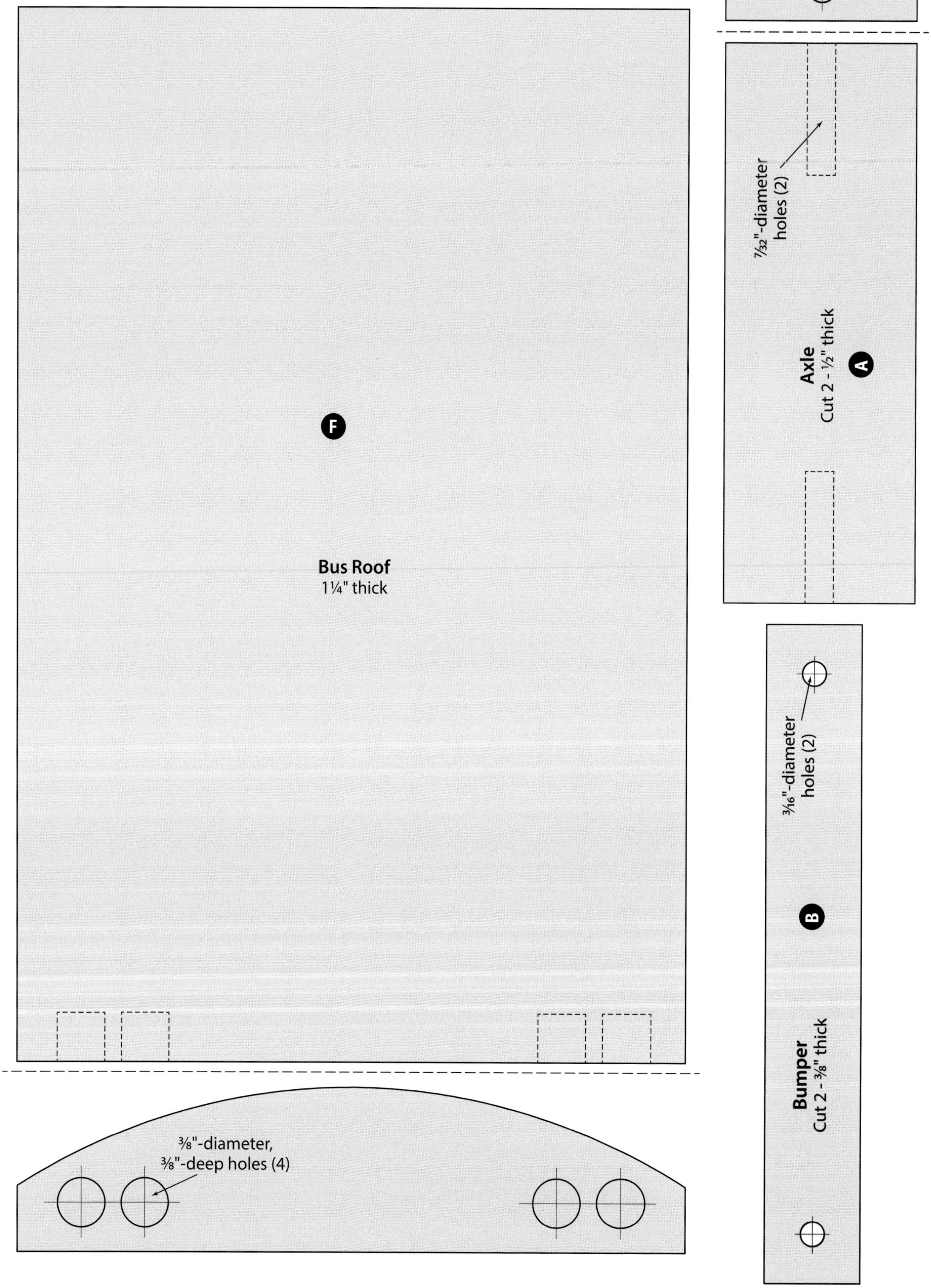

Index

Note: Page numbers in *italics* indicate projects (and patterns in parentheses).

Acknowledgments

First and foremost, I would like to acknowledge the love and support from my wife, Katie. In our early days of dating, she spent a day with me in the garage, hand-sanding toys I had made for a local charity. Since then, she has continued to support me in the countless hours I spend in the garage each weekend. She is a sounding board for new ideas and has always encouraged me to follow my dreams. She is truly my better half.

My three children—Kyle, Joshua, and Derek—were my inspiration for designing toys that would last, even with the roughest play. They were my original toy testers.

I would like to thank Kaylee Schofield, editor at Fox Chapel Publishing, for giving me the opportunity to create this book. Her advice and encouragement have played an integral part in its development.

In addition to Kaylee, the team at *Scroll Saw Woodworking & Crafts* magazine has allowed me the opportunity to write and share my designs with a wider audience.

Finally, nothing brings me more joy than seeing a child play with a toy that I created. I would like to thank all the charitable organizations who still accept handmade toys and help bring joy to children everywhere.

About the Author

Brad Anderson is a continuous improvement engineer with a degree in mechanical engineering. His passion for design is evident in his hobby of creating and crafting toys. Several of his designs have been featured in *Scroll Saw Woodworking & Crafts* magazine. Additionally, he dedicates time to making toys that he donates to local charitable organizations.